DATE DUE

Three Portraits

HITLER
MUSSOLINI
STALIN

AMS PRESS
NEW YORK

Three Portraits

HITLER
MUSSOLINI
STALIN

by Emil Ludwig

ALLIANCE BOOK CORPORATION
LONGMANS, GREEN AND COMPANY
NEW YORK AND TORONTO

Library of Congress Cataloging in Publication Data

Ludwig, Emil, 1881–1948.
  Three portraits.

  Reprint. Originally published: New York: Alliance
Book Corp., Longmans, Green, 1940.
  1. Hitler, Adolf, 1889–1945. 2. Mussolini, Benito,
1883–1945. 3. Stalin, Joseph, 1879–1953. 4. Heads of
State—Europe—Biography. 5. Europe—Politics and
government—20th century. I. Title. II. Title: Hitler,
Mussolini, Stalin.
D412.7.L82 1982   940.5 [B]   78-63689
ISBN 0-404-16905-8   AACR2

Reprinted from the edition of 1940, New York. Trim size and text
area have been altered. Original trim: 14 × 21.5 cm.; original
text: 9.7 × 15.6 cm.

MANUFACTURED
IN THE UNITED STATES OF AMERICA

FOREWORD

PORTRAITS OF CONTEMPORARIES CANNOT BREATHE THAT air of calm we try to give portraits of the past. An impartial "History of our own Times" is neither possible nor desirable. It is precisely because of their prejudice that the greatest histories, the works of Xenophon or Tacitus on their own epoch, are so interesting today. At the same time, there is a great difference between a personal view and partisanship. Only one who feels himself as free of party feeling and interest as the present writer can hope to attain, in the midst of war, that degree of platonic detachment which he owes to himself and his readers in view of his former work.

Two of the European dictators I know from personal conversations, the third by description. I am against all three, because they are all against freedom. Like everybody else, however, I am interested in their characters, since our fate today depends in part on them. I have always sought authority for my views, and in these portraits diverge from those already published at few points only.

5

After the war the whole glamor of dictatorship which has ensnared the world of today will vanish like other maladies.

These three personalities are as various as their aims, yet in both aspects the order of merit is not identical. In the following pages, the aims of Stalin will be seen to be more interesting than those of the other two. Mussolini, on the other hand, is the most interesting personality. The reader is invited to check this presentation by his own opinion. To a booklet of this kind, discussion is as welcome as agreement.

E. L.

Moscia, February 1940,
(Switzerland).

CONTENTS

One: HITLER

One: HITLER

OF ALL THE FAMOUS MEN OF OUR DAY, NONE looks so insignificant as Adolf Hitler. Roosevelt represents the best type of American; no one would take him for a Frenchman, a doctor or a clergyman. Mussolini, with his Caesarean head is at the first glance the Roman dictator. Even Stalin has the expression of a coherent personality.

Hitler looks neither German nor a statesman; least of all is he typical of the race he worships. Max von Gruber, a Professor at the University of Munich, and the most eminent eugenist in Germany, stated as a witness in the law court in 1923: "It was the first time I had seen Hitler close at hand. Face and head of inferior type, cross-breed; low receding forehead, ugly nose, broad cheekbones, little eyes, dark hair. Expression not of a man exercising authority in perfect self-command, but of raving excitement. At the end an expression of satisfied egotism."

Nothing we see in his portrait, his habits, his style

would be of the least interest, if the whole were not pervaded by that "raving excitement" emphasized by the scientist, which is the sole explanation of his success. A pathological being, who, like many others in history, has translated the diseased exaggeration of certain impulses into a self-importance which is the source of his decisions and actions. This temperamental heat, this gambling trait in his character distinguishes him from Mussolini, who is cold and cynical. The link between genius and madness, so frequent a subject of research, stands out at the supreme moments of Hitler's life. It is that which makes him incalculable, and if, after the great débâcle, he were to stand on trial before a world tribunal, it is even open to question whether serious alienists would pronounce him responsible. By that we can measure the worth of his treaties or his promises.

The main traits of his restless, fitful character are already evident in his early life. He was imbued with the passionate wish to make up for a bad start; there is no trace of any determination to lay the foundation of a steady happiness, no trace of love for any one, parents, family or women. What stands out clearly is his hatred of anything standing higher in the world's eyes than himself. Even his father spent his whole life living down his illegitimate birth and the honest cobbler's craft to which he had been trained, and striving to become a state employee with a peaked cap, a title and a pension. Till his death, the obscure Bohemian customs officer struggled to

Hitler

cut a figure in his little provincial home town, to be somebody; he even discarded his mother's name—which was Schicklgruber—and took that of his mother-in-law. His three marriages were inspired by the same desire, so that, in order to rise in the world, he took as his first wife a woman fourteen years his senior, as his third a girl twenty-three years his junior, who became Hitler's mother.

The son inherited his father's resentment. Instead of taking seriously to the schooling his mother's savings put within his reach, he left school at fourteen, on account of lung trouble at first, later for no reason at all. He passed his entire youth without making the least attempt to acquire any knowledge or trade. As he himself writes: "As the breach widened between my ideal and the secondary school curriculum, my inward indifference grew. Everything I neglected in my defiance at school I had to pay for bitterly later." He states in his book that even then he could endure no compulsion to regular hours of work or tasks, but wished to become a free artist, a painter. "Very well," said the poor mother. "Try the Academy of Art in Vienna." Once in Vienna, however, he was turned down for lack of ability, and was not even allowed to make a second attempt. The architectural school, which he tried next, would not admit him, since he had neither a school certificate, nor the natural gifts to substitute for it. His pride still smarts from these failures. When his mother died immediately afterward, he found himself at twenty in the streets of Vienna, penniless and without any apparent aptitude or training for any kind of useful work.

For the next four years, the best training period for a young man with a goal in the world, Hitler lived, aimless and idle, on the charity of rich, mostly Jewish organizations,—first in an institution for the homeless, then in a Men's Home. That was in 1910, when there was no unemployment problem. From time to time he would earn a few pennies as an outside porter; from time to time he might shovel some snow. He got his meals in the soup kitchens for the poor, provided by the Jewish Baron Königswarter. The only effort he made to support himself was to paint postcards or copy pictures which a friend sold for him to dealers and to a furniture maker, who inserted the pictures as inlays in the backs of sofas.

Hanisch, the artist, who at twenty was Hitler's friend for nearly a year, and acted as go-between in the sale of his wares, speaks kindly of him in his memoirs. One of Hitler's sketches made at the time shows two postmen, one of whom is almost prostrated by the heat and is wringing out his stockings, while the other looks on cheerfully, recommending a perspiration powder in rhyme. This advertisement was drawn for the Hungarian Jew, Neumann, who gave him money, shirts and a so-called *Kaiserrock*. At the time Hitler spoke of him with the greatest gratitude. Invariably wearing his long coat, his unshaven chin covered with dark bristles he was nicknamed "Uncle Kruger," after the President of the Boers.

Intellectually, Hitler was attracted in Vienna by the anti-Semitism which the Mayor was then developing into a political program. It was directed against the numerous Viennese Jews, many of whom were at the head of many business houses, and sought no other justification than the struggle against competition. Hitler, like all innately indolent characters, welcomed passionately any class of people he could blame by word or deed, for blocking his way in the world. He joined this aggressive party because he saw many rich Jews in Vienna. But that did not prevent him from living on Jewish charity; indeed, for years after, he painted a New Year card for the Jewish family doctor, and sent it from Vienna to Linz signed: "In deep gratitude, Adolf Hitler."

By thus making himself dependent on a race whose influence he both exaggerated and envied, his innate weakness bred a hatred of those to whom, in spite of theory, he ought to have felt grateful. In the Men's Home, moreover, he had met certain individual disreputable Jews, and judged the race by the individuals. We would be no less wrong and equally justified in judging the Germans by Hitler.

With the organizational gifts Hitler later displayed, he could not have helped making his way in the world as a young man, even without credentials, if his repulsion for any kind of regular work had not become an affliction. He had the so-called "artist's dream," which his lack of talent made it impossible for him to fulfill. For such a young man, determined to rise in the world at all costs, there is only one way—politics, and in politics, the movements he finds open to him. As Hitler says of himself, he read at the time some pamphlets on the Greater Germany and the social politics of the day, learned their claptrap and in the course of long debates with other idle inmates of the Home, discovered that he was a better debater than most. He was, of course, not yet an orator, but his wild and hot-headed way of shouting the others down, his gestures, above all the acrimonious passion of his speeches, stemming from his deeply-rooted envy of all who drove past in fine clothes and fine cars, who lived in rich apartments or had the right to enter a box at the opera, gave him an advantage over the others and made up for coherent reasoning.

Bit by bit he learned the arguments for the anti-Semitism then in vogue in Vienna. At the same time, although baptized a Catholic, he became a furious opponent of the Catholic Church, which the very men who were blaming the Jews for all the misfortunes of Austria, were striving to annihilate in the so-called "Away from Rome" movement. The third plank in their party's platform was the union of Austria with Prussia, and Hitler confessed the enthusiasm he felt when, under the rule of the Hapsburg Emperors, a member of the Viennese Parliament shouted: "Long live Hohenzollern." The status of Germany as a great power attracted this son of Austria as irresistibly as everything else in the world which radiated position, influence, brilliance.

In the idleness of his youth, he looked about for pinnacles to be climbed by some ladder or other, as yet unknown. While in his pro-German enthusiasm, he was one of the small group of "Anschluss" partisans, in the debates in the Home he thundered against the Socialists, to whom, as a variety of "worker," he nevertheless belonged. Like his father, Hitler's first ambition was to ascend to the middle class. Counts and princes were beyond his range; he did not envy them. Workmen were wretched creatures; he avoided them. But the middle class, the secure middle class, that was his ideal, and since most Jews were neither nobles nor workmen, aristocrats nor proletariat, plutocrats nor paupers, but safe in the middle class, and many of them supreme there, he found another reason for hating them.

Suddenly the War saved the self-deluded artist, who had finally tried his luck in Munich with the same lack of success. Hating everything that marked his origin, his country, his class, his parents and family (who are not even mentioned in his memoirs) he enlisted as a volunteer in the German Army in order to avoid military service in Austria. There, for the first time in his life, he formed part of a huge community, the German Army. An aim, a goal stood before him, namely, to do his part in defending the German Empire and its people. At the declaration of war, he writes, he sank weeping on his knees. Since, however, it is his habit to explain every reaction in the world around him by his own, he declares in his memoirs that the whole

German people desired the War simply because he desired it himself.

In the four years he spent on the Western Front, Hitler was once slightly wounded and once gassed. The gassing affects his voice even today and necessitates caution in eating and drinking. An exhaustive examination of all the documents and witnesses of Hitler's war service has shown that he spent the whole four years on orderly duty with the regimental staff, and that that staff lost but a single man in the entire war. According to the German textbooks for use in schools, he was awarded the Iron Cross, First Class, for a brilliant feat, namely, for having surprised from twelve to fifteen Frenchmen in a trench and delivering them all as prisoners to the regimental commander. In the history of the regiment, which describes two similar incidents with names and dates, there is not one word of this story. Whether he was really awarded the Iron Cross has never been proved. It is unlikely, to say the least.

It is noteworthy that he remained a lance corporal for the whole of the four years. Although there was an insufficient number of sergeants, his company commander declared at the time: "I shall never promote that lunatic." In his speeches, Hitler later conferred upon himself the title of "The Unknown Soldier of the World War." Unfortunately, it is the real hero that is now lying in his tomb of honor in Berlin.

After the War, a host of secret societies arose, with the approval and partial direction of the Reichswehr, to arm the German people against—and in violation of—the Treaty of Versailles. A few army officers recognized the oratorical gift of Lance Corporal Hitler, who had now returned from the front, and made use of him as an agitator. When he became involved in a political trial, the Reichswehr reluctantly dropped him. In Munich, Hitler joined one of the recently formed party clubs which later became the Nazi party, and rapidly developed as a popular orator between 1919 and 1923. He took lessons in public speaking from an actor and so improved his oratory that he was soon able to hold thousands under his spell. Here we have the first source of his success.

The Germans are perhaps the only nation which has never had a great popular orator. Music and oratory are seldom found together, whether in men or in nations. Thus it is not surprising that the English, an unmusical nation as a whole, have produced the most outstanding political orators, while the Germans, who lead the world in music, have produced none. As German ministers were appointed by their kings and princes, and not taken from the parliaments, they had no training in public speaking. Bismarck, for example, delivered a public address for the first time at the age of 77, after his dismissal.

Hitler's technique of oratory is largely the result of his study of mass psychology, into which he delved passionately after the war. He declared to his small, new party that everything depended on fascinating the crowd. Above all, he realized the one thing the German Republicans had neglected, namely, to restore to the German people, deprived of an army, their flags, bands and songs. An admirer of Richard Wagner, from whom he learned the technique of parades, choruses and heroic poses, Hitler displayed far more imagination than his predecessors in the Republic, although it was an imagination of the crudest type. He invented every emblem himself, except the swastika, designed his own flag, and prescribed every collar and button for the slowly-growing party troops.

The swastika he imported from Finland, where German soldiers had seen it in their campaign of intervention after the war. The swastika originated in Asia, and the Finns, who are partly descended from the Mongols, brought it from Mongolia. The Party which regards the German race as supreme, bears as its badge the emblem of an alien, colored tribe.

Hitler's main aim was to attract attention to *himself*. From the very beginning, he personally arranged all the lighting effects and spotlights, as well as his entry into a hall with fanfares. He trained crowds to salute with the right arm, taught them his songs, and transformed the audience from an apathetic mass into active collaborators in his festivities.

As a stage manager and advertiser, he gave proof of real genius. In his book, thirty-two pages are devoted to the War, twenty of which are occupied with the question of propaganda which, as he says, the Germans had managed badly. "The Entente," he writes, "won the war simply and solely by its propaganda." A crowd is ready to believe anything, "true or false," provided it is constantly reiterated; one has only to say the same thing often enough. He is past-master in the technique of platform speaking, and can be humorous, grave, witty, tragic and cynical as the occasion requires. He is at his best in the great crescendo from a grave, gloomy beginning to the invective in which his voice breaks and he begins to scream. His effect, in complete contrast to Mussolini's, is due to the fact that he juggles with mystical notions such as Honor, Blood and Soil, and thus wraps his audience in that cloud of mysticism which the Germans love far more than mere prosaic logic. In this manner he has won thousands of hearts, especially the women's, because he works to create the single great impression that here is a prophet whose heart is bleeding for the fate of his people. His shrill, hysterical cries are primarily genuine; Hitler talks himself into a paroxysm. Yet at the same time he is sly enough to use an arrangement on his speaker's desk through which, by pressing a button, the spotlights are switched on to him so that his ecstasies can be properly filmed for the news reels. A similar combination of ecstasy and artifice can be observed in other actors.

Five years after the end of the war, Hitler thought he could risk a *coup d'état* with his young party. He joined forces with Ludendorff, the German commander in the World War. Part of the Bavarian Reichswehr was on his side, but the Prussians in Berlin were solid in opposition.

On Armistice Day, 1923, he risked a *putsch* in the Bür-
gerbräu in Munich, with the object of overthrowing the
German Republic from Bavaria. That night, during a
gigantic mass meeting, he very cleverly trapped General
Ludendorff and some of the ministers in a room, and
with drawn revolver, forced them to surrender and cooperate with him. Most of them, however, abandoned him
later. Thereupon he commanded over a hundred of his
armed adherents to make an open attack on the armed
police force. The latter met the rebels' attack in a narrow
Munich street. Shots were fired. Fourteen men lay dead
on the Munich pavement. At that moment, Hitler vanished
in a car.

His trial as the instigator of the rising brought all these
circumstances clearly to light. While Hitler decamped by
car during the first minutes of his first fight, General
Ludendorff walked straight up to the rifles, and passed
between them, confident that nobody would dare to fire
on him. The first fourteen heroes of the Nazi movement
were later eulogized solemnly and magnificently at the
scene of their death, by the leader who had abandoned
them in danger. Five years later, Hitler came into a meeting
in the same hall leading a boy by the hand, and stated that
he had jumped into the car to save the boy's life. No boy
had appeared at the trial, and even then nobody knew him.

After the failure of his *coup d'état* and the dissolution of
his party, Hitler proved his passionate perseverance to rise
in the world by maintaining an unflinching faith in his

mission. He began once again, from another side. He spent a year as a political prisoner in a fortress where he enjoyed every comfort except permission to leave. This "imprisonment," of which he made great play in the development of the Hitler legend, was as different from the concentration camps he set up later as a Pullman drawing room from a cattle truck. It was there, too, that he began to write his book, though its crucial chapters, those against France, were not written until 1926. Therefore they were not written, as his partisans declare, under the fresh impression of the French occupation of the Ruhr, which came to an end in 1923. The grotesque German in which the book is written points to Hitler himself as its actual author.

In the eight years that followed, between the ages of 36 and 44, he reconstructed his party and displayed his brilliant talents as an organizer, for which the German character provides such admirable material. He realized that he could rise only through the support of the discontented and utterly disillusioned middle class. Hitler never convinced or won over the working class. All he did later was to subjugate it. Rauschning describes in detail Hitler's intense hatred of Germany's laboring masses. Born in the lower middle class, Hitler comprehended its mentality and won it to his side. To these people who had been deprived of their former self-confidence, he restored pride in themselves in the form of titles, uniforms and parades. Anyone, by joining his party, could flatter his self-importance with a badge, and become, if not leader of a group, at least a deputy-assistant-party-group-treasurer in his village. The pyramid familiar to the Germans, that structure in which each individual carries another on his back but makes up for it by standing on somebody else, was set up anew by Hitler. The Germans, who love order more than freedom, and whose ruling passion is obedience, rejoiced in their release from an uncomfortable equality into new ranks of superiors and inferiors. This is the second source of Hitler's success.

Although he had to hold his ground against dozens of competitors from other new parties, all of whom were out to restore to the German people their place in the sun, Hitler, with his party, succeeded in eliminating them all. As the best speaker, he attracted the largest numbers. As a man without religion, without philosophy, without principles, he balked at nothing. While he reiterated to himself and others that his sole object was to restore the German people, he concealed from himself and others his desire for self-aggrandizement, and today at last—believes in his own idealism.

Since the banks and the big industrialists wished to rid themselves of the Socialists, with their wage demands and strikes, they contributed generously to this popular party. It was even in the interests of the Reichswehr to be on good terms with the young party, since Hitler's speeches constantly promised the masses a renewal of the soldier-spirit, a new army and new victories. The bitter experience of his first, abortive rising, however, had warned Hitler against any repetition of an act of violence. He was now determined to win power by a majority only, and even against the opinion of his friends, obstinately clung to his decision to get the government "legally" into his hands. After five years of a propaganda campaign such as the world has never seen, he succeeded, in 1930, in sending 110 deputies to the Reichstag, forming the strongest party. And through legislative means, he brought pressure to bear on the President of the Reich and isolated him. Hindenburg despised Hitler because he was a General and Hitler a corporal, because he was a Junker and Hitler a plebeian, because he was a Prussian and Hitler an Austrian. For years he kept him at bay. The story of how he was taken by assault is told in my book on Hindenburg. The upshot was that the old man, then over eighty, fell victim to an intrigue and imagined he was appointing a chancellor who would rule along with the other parties under his own presidency. When on January 30, 1933 he appeared side by side with Adolf Hitler on the balcony in the Wilhelmstrasse, cheerfully whistling the march which was being played below in the light of a thousand torches, he had no inkling of the march of events he had set going that day, and for which he stands responsible in the eyes of history.

II

Dictatorship, even in its German form, is devoid of humor. The basic reason why Americans will never endure a dictator is, in my opinion, their sense of humor. A man who is always sunk in gloom, who can speak to his people only with resounding emotion, would be merely a ludicrous figure to the American people, with their innate common sense. The Italians and Germans have their own forms of humor, but humor does not pervade their lives. If we compare the parliamentary reports of the various countries, we shall see "laughter" most frequently noted in the speeches delivered in Washington and London, less often in Paris, and least of all in the reports from Rome and Berlin in the days when they still had parliaments. Both nations love tragedy and have no great comedy. In America the careers of popular presidents are highlighted with jokes and pranks. The man who takes himself too seriously here is hopelessly lost as a public figure.

The Germans, as Clemenceau once said, are in love with death. Even their humor is of a melancholic nature, arising from the mysticism of their general outlook, which, in its turn, is connected subjectively with their passion for music. All of these traits appear in their individualism, which is predominant in all intellectual and spiritual questions. The cleavage between the spiritual and political life of the nation has made the Germans intellectual hermits, while at the same time, making them an obedient unit in the State.

That is why it has always been so easy for mediocre minds to become the political leaders of Germany, and so difficult for great minds. Bismarck was ardently hated in his country until he was rudely thrown out of office by an arrogant young Kaiser. Great generals, such as Scharnhorst or Moltke, and outstanding statesmen, such as Humboldt and Freiherr von Stein, were never popular. Dull saber rattlers like General Wrangel, Field Marshal Blücher, or Field Marshal Hindenburg, on the other hand, have always been beloved. Men with trained minds, such as Bethmann-Hollweg or Rathenau were, as Ministers, under suspicion from the outset in Germany. Scholarship, they feel, belongs in a university. It is not the pen, but the sword which rules. In government, all that matters is browbeating manifestoes, the drawn sword, the ready fist. That is why Germany has never had a first-class politician in the government except Bismarck, and very rarely any in the opposition.

Hitler, who had made his way to power by his great gifts as a stage manager and speaker, introduced into the Reichschancellory all that browbeating noise which the Germans are so prone to take for greatness. All that Hitler lacked, the Germans were persuaded to imagine by his disciple Goebbels. Immediately after his appointment as Chancellor, Hitler resolved to prove to the world that he had come, a new Saint George, to slay the dragon of communism. While the German Reichstag was burning, he accused the Communists of the guilt, and when none would believe it, was forced into a public trial before the Court of the Reich. This trial he lost, morally speaking, for its sole result was to expose the guilt of the Nazis.

The day on which Hindenburg died was still more important for him. That day, August 2, 1934, was the most perilous and greatest of Hitler's career. For a year and a half he had been ruling as Reichschancellor. He had crushed every other party, and his governmental superior, the President, had been on his side. At the President's death he had, according to the constitution, to reckon with the general election of a new President, and then with his own provisional resignation. He had long speculated as to how long Hindenburg, then 85, would live; the aged President's two doctors had given different opinions.

Three men were being groomed by their adherents as Hindenburg's successor, Field Marshal von Mackensen, Hindenburg's son, and the former Crown Prince. Hitler could not but fear that he had lost his game a second time. It was a terrible situation. The two appalling days of slaughter, June 30, 1934, when he had his recalcitrant party members massacred, and July 25th, when he had organized the assassination of the Austrian Chancellor Dollfuss, were hardly past.

When the aged Hindenburg lay finally dying, Hitler flew immediately from Bayreuth to the death bed. He then held a cabinet meeting in Berlin, and had an act passed which bears the date of August 1, 1934, the eve, that is, of Hindenburg's death. In this act, Hitler was appointed Hindenburg's successor, and given the right to nominate his deputy. "This act enters into force at the moment of the demise of President Hindenburg." In this way he eliminated the risk entailed in the prescribed general election, and had himself made head of the State by his own henchmen. Everything now depended on whether the generals would accept such an act of constitutional mayhem.

The generals were won over. Probably by prearrangement, General von Blomberg, then Minister of War, took up Hitler's cause in a proclamation to the people. The General even spontaneously conferred upon Hitler a new title, hailing him in the proclamation as "Führer of the German Reich and People." On that day the German Army took its oath to a head of state with a non-existent title. When all was over, Hitler ordered a plebiscite in which the German people were allowed to confirm the usurpation of their supreme rights.

To make quite sure of the plebiscite, a will of Hindenburg's had to be produced. But on August 13th, eleven days after his death, the existence of such a will was known neither to his own son nor to Meissner, the Secretary of State. Suddenly, four days before the plebiscite, a newly discovered will made its appearance, which the *London Times* called "just as important as the burning of the Reichstag." No one has ever seen it. It has never been photographed. The place of its discovery and the reasons for its belated "appearance" have never been divulged.

Fully half of it consists of a long passage lifted bodily from Hindenburg's memoirs, the other half, of the expressed wish that the German people might continue to prosper by the movement of my "Chancellor, Adolf Hitler." This was emphasized in a broadcast on the eve of the plebiscite by Hindenburg's son, who stated that his father had regarded Hitler as his immediate successor in the leadership of the German people. The will was no more genuine than the guilt of the Communists for the burning of the Reichstag.

In spite of all these tricks, more than five million Germans rejected Hitler on that day. In view of the strict supervision of the "secret" ballot, this may be considered a demonstration of decency on the part of those Germans not yet in bondage.

III

In spite of all his acts of violence, Hitler has unquestionably brought material success to the German people. But what, specifically, has Hitler given the Germans?

Commands and a Sword. Since they are the only people in history who obey with passion, and not compulsion, they felt uneasy in the fourteen years of freedom they had just enjoyed for the first time in centuries. They were unhappy without their drill sergeants to give them orders. When Hitler, in his speech on May 1, 1938, hurled the word "obedience" at them three times in a row, the ether fairly quivered with the surge of enthusiasm provoked by the word.

He gave the Germans the Sword—a figure of speech, of course. The German sword, which had been wrested from their hands by a victorious enemy and was now restored to them by Hitler, was for that warlike people the great gift, the final fulfillment of a great longing. For three hundred years, and especially for the last fifty, uniforms had been admired on the streets of Germany. The lieutenant had been the romantic hero of all the girls; decorations, parades, flags, epitomized all the glory of life. For fourteen years such "glory" had been only a memory; because years are required to re-equip a defeated people, materially or spiritually,—because the leaders of the Republic lacked imagination. But when every barber's boy got back his helmet and every bootblack his wellingtons, the heart of the soldier-people rejoiced. Today there are more riding boots in Germany than on the pampas. But there are very few riders.

It was Richard Wagner who restored the symbolic meaning to the German Sword. When the audience first watched Siegmund draw it out of the ash tree, in the "Valkyrie," every heart thrilled. Because such ideas are incompatible with the teachings of the Gospel, the fight against the Bible in present-day Germany is perfectly logical. The Germans were wretched so long as they had no Sword. The acclaim of the post-war world for their inventions, their Zeppelins, for their great musicians, physicists and writers, was powerless to satisfy their pride. Only a world once more trembling before the gigantic, armored juggernaut of a German army could do that. We cannot deny that a genuine idealism—of sorts—inspires the

German Nazi youth. It is bellicose, prepared for any event, and looks forward to a hero's death. At present, the Nazi youth really desires neither peace nor personal happiness. They demand sacrifice for the community, the victory of the idea of Germany. As others believe in God, they believe in the superiority of the German race and in its right to rule the world.

Their new leader did not merely promise them all this; he began to turn it into reality before their very eyes. By the Treaty of Versailles, the German Reich lost six million inhabitants in Europe; under Hitler it has gained 40 million, and a conquered territory rich in raw materials. The German Republic had inherited the Rhineland, the Saar district and Austria as German territories; it had been unable to keep them. The rape of Czecho-Slovakia was the first thing to actually estrange all democrats from nazism. The fact that the rape was accomplished by threats alone reveals the weakness of the adversary, but it also shows the superior tactical talent of the German Führer. The technique of Government by advertisement, hitherto confined mainly to business life, has enabled a ruler of our day to attain his aims by sheer propaganda and bluff, instead of by the time-honored negotiation procedure. The rapid action of a dictatorship here reveals its technical superiority over the slowness of a government under popular control.

These huge external triumphs, the increase in raw material sources and the strength of the army, which Hitler has reaped for Germany in the course of six years, were attained by methods which, at first sight, had an excellent effect within the country. There was employment for thousands in the vast armament works into which Germany was transformed. The industrialists earned their millions, the worker his daily wage. In the very first months of his office, Hitler took four million out of the ranks of the unemployed and made them build guns, tanks, planes, warships and forts. Thousands of retired officers who had never learned anything but the preparation and conduct of warfare, were at last restored to their positions and their incomes. During years of very skillful reorganization, Hitler managed to reconcile his private army with the new Army of the People, and at the same time to ensure the integrity of his own bodyguard.

What he asked from the people in return,—self-denial and frugality in food, cheap clothes and poor housing— would have been given so gladly by no other people. The enthusiasm of the Germans when the honor of their Army was restored, the employment of millions in the rearmament process, their innate will to obey, their great frugality,—all contributed to ease the way for this resolute man. Time, too, was on his side, for the lean post-war years were long past. Hitler's declaration that communism was at Germany's door at his accession to power is a fabrication; the last Communist rising had taken place eight years before.

Nor need Hitler have had any real fear of the former

enemy. The three great burdens of the Treaty of Versailles had been peacefully cleared out of the way by Stresemann, Rathenau and Brüning long before his day. The occupation of the Rhineland had been peacefully discussed, the question of reparations had been settled, while the strength of the Reichswehr was to be increased to 300,000. Hitler might well assume that nobody would prevent him from rearming, since a secret rearmament had been begun long before.

The question, however, was whether the former Entente would sit back and allow him to march into the Rhineland. In this situation he showed his masterly knowledge of public opinion. He refused to be concerned about treaties. He relied confidently on the natural peaceableness of his neighbors, which would prevent them from stopping his march into the prohibited zone fifteen years after the end of the War. Hitler and Goebbels had their agents in France and England, and followed public sentiment in those countries through their detailed reports. When I asked a famous French general in 1936 the reasons for France's apparent indifference during Hitler's coup, he replied: "In France no President can mobilize the army without being attacked!" Since the French had made the mistake of talking incessantly for fifteen years about their security and love of peace, without making an occasional threat, the Germans realized that all their neighbor wanted was to possess his own garden and reap its fruits. All he would do would be to look over the hedge and ask politely

to be left in peace. For fifteen years the English had believed that it was the French that desired conquest, and
not the Germans. They took the Germans for gentlemen,
that is, for Englishmen, and considered the French to be
warlike. If men like Clemenceau and Churchill had been
at the head of affairs in Paris and London, Hitler would
have seen his not yet rearmed country invaded, and he
would have been overthrown at home in 1935. The Bald-
wins and Chamberlains refused to run any risk of war,
especially as they realized the connection between war
and great social changes, while the Americans could not
be aroused for any reason at all. They declared, and quite
rightly: If the Rhineland, the Saar district, or Austria are
really going to be inhabited by Germans, why should we
go to war five thousand miles away to stop the Germans
from annexing those German territories?

The Hitler triumphs were won both by the moral
weakness of his neighbors, and by the unscrupulousness of
his actions. His method of bringing pressure to bear on
elections was as new as the promptitude of his actions. A
friend once related to me what he had heard from the
widow of Troost, the builder. Soon after the occupation
of the Rhineland, Hitler, who had been a friend of her
husband's in the old Munich days, came to her, saying,
"I've been sweating blood these two days for fear they
would march after all. Now it's done. Now all they can
do is to talk it down!"

That is the language of a gambler—of a man who

stakes his all on one card, in the firm belief that, when the other players simply refuse to call a bluff, he may safely risk his stake.

And yet, with the great triumphs Hitler has flaunted before his people year after year, with the increase of power and population that cost him not a single man, how are we to explain the apathy shared by all Germans, with the exception of the few thousands commandeered to function at processions? They do not revolt, yet they are neither happy nor content. When the vigorous will of one man has won so many visible triumphs in six years, when he has again made his country the terror of its neighbors, and as though such triumphs never occurred, the enthusiasm of the country wanes instead of waxing—as it has been since the third year of the Hitler régime—there must be deep-rooted reasons for it. What are those reasons?

IV

The first reason is the indignation aroused by the acts of violence which were committed not only in the first weeks of the new régime, but which have become increasingly frequent for the last six years. When Hitler had 1100 people shot on June 30, 1934, without trial or sentence, a cry of horror was raised throughout the civilized world. The fact that his best friends were among the massacred shows the evil potentialities of the man. Field Marshal Hindenburg had to send his Chancellor a telegram of thanks for the slaughter. It was almost the last document he ever signed; he died a month later.

Then, as now, death sentences and imprisonments rained down upon the ranks of his political opponents. All the old parties, which Hitler solemnly promised to respect on his accession to power, he has battered to pieces. The Germans, accustomed to fixed legal concepts, looked on with horror while a gang of lawless barbarians wrought havoc about them, secure in the force of their weapons.

The second cause of resentment is the fight against the Church. The Germans had accepted the persecution of the Jews, having always been anti-Semitic in feeling. We have proof that not only S. A. men, acting under orders, but also university professors took part in the pogroms. Fourteen thousand Jews had been allowed to die for their country. And now their names were removed from the war memorials.

Christianity had meant much less to later generations in Germany than it had to England or the United States. There were no theological debates there, no interpretations of Scripture, no quarrels between sects. Yet the Church was there, people went to it, it formed part of family life. Its influence has been destroyed by the intervention of the State, the significance of marriage has rapidly diminished, the young revolt against the old.

And then there are the martyrs. The young Communists, thousands of whom sacrificed their lives for their freedom, do not belong to the lower middle classes which dominate Germany by the example of their Führer. But the cardinals, bishops and priests of both creeds, who are steadfastly defending the Bible against the State, bring back to people's minds the one successful revolution Germany has seen—Luther's. That struggle, the trial of Pastor Niemöller and the imprisonment of four thousand of the clergy, ravage public opinion.

The third reason is the private life of a large number of the leaders. Hitler himself has been praised for his asceticism; any simplicity is confined to his stomach, and only because his stomach trouble compels him to be careful about his food. It is no secret that the forced sale of three million copies of his book, *Mein Kampf*, at two dollars apiece, has made him a rich man, and that he controls the largest publishing house of the Third Reich, which was founded by his friends. It is true that Prince Bismarck sold his memoirs to his publisher for a million marks, and Prince Bülow sold his for half a million. Yet both books appeared after their death, so that their sales could not have increased through fear of or respect for their writers. Hitler has made himself a millionaire, and hence waives his official salary. The luxury of his country houses and estates, his private forests and game preserves, the silver and jewels acquired or stolen by other party leaders were the talk of the world even before Knickerbocker's revelations made the foreign investments of the "saviors of Germany" public property.

The fourth cause of bitterness is the impotence of intellectual Germany. We, the "burnt authors," receive letter after letter from old readers complaining that our books are no longer allowed into Germany. Men of learning, doctors, journalists and philosophers are finding it very bitter indeed, never to be allowed to write what they know to be the truth. That intellectual Germany submitted very quickly—the last German professor took his oath at the end of eight weeks—can be explained by the sufferings to which the Germans had been forced to submit by their defeat, and the harsh peace terms, which they hoped at last to cast off. Within a short time they realized that, having hitherto been dependent on powers outside the country, they were now subjected to a power at home whose barbarism appalled them. It was precisely the scholars occupied in research on racial questions, such as Professor Günther, philosophers like Spengler who had prophesied the resurrection of Germany, who now repudiated the violence which has replaced ethics. The appointment of ignorant young men by the Party to high places in German universities and clinics, once so famous, has caused profound depression in the country of Goethe and Kant.

The last and deepest cause of resentment of millions of people is general uncertainty as to the law. A country which no longer recognizes a written constitution, a country in which the Minister of Justice proclaims as his guiding principle, "Right is what is useful to Germany," a country in which the police force is recruited only from the ruling Party, and which watches with sympathetic

interest any crime which is committed to the Party's advantage—is a country where none can feel safe. Even the
free can hardly take much pleasure in life in a country
where more than 100,000 souls are imprisoned in camps
without a trial, forced to sleep on sacks of straw in un-
heated rooms because their ideas of God and the State
do not tally with those of the ruling Party. Each man
dreads that his neighbor may denounce him; no man dares
to speak aloud in public. All letters are at the mercy of the
Party censors, not a telephone conversation is private, not
a word can be printed which displeases those in power.
Anyone tuned in to a prohibited radio station is hauled
off to prison.

The general feeling of insecurity is enhanced by the
indignity of such a life. Any German who has not risen
to wealth and position through the Party feels far less free
than he did under the Treaty of Versailles. Then, his rifle
was taken from him but not his right to free speech; if he
felt like cursing his German ministers, he could also curse
the Treaty. Millions are ashamed because they are no
longer citizens of a constitutional State.

V

Meanwhile their Führer sits in his villa in the Bavarian
mountains. To this villa he summons his ministers, because
he no longer feels safe in Berlin, and here he entertains his
friends. He is never seen before ten in the morning. His

ministers often have to wait till noon. As he talks ceaselessly and seldom listens, he frequently holds forth on a single subject for an hour and a half, so that other business cannot be settled.

His amusements are the cinema, where he may sit through three films on a single evening, and the visits of film actors and actresses, to whom he talks for whole evenings of his frustrated passion—art. His few affairs with women have all come to a sudden end.

All his relations with women were short-lived, as Konrad Heiden points out in his excellent biography. Erna Hanfstaengl, the sister of Hitler's first political crony, Ernst Hanfstaengl, whom he banished some time after his accession to power, did not return his passion. From about 1926-1928 she was a well-known figure in Munich society, but her American grandmother was the Jewish Mrs. Heim. The *Völkischer Beobachter* published a denial of any affair; Hitler, it said, was not engaged to Miss Hanfstaengl. The truth of the matter was that she preferred the celebrated surgeon Sauerbruch of Munich, who was shortly afterwards called to the University of Berlin.

In 1931-1932, Hitler was often a guest of Siegfried Wagner's widow, Frau Winifred Wagner in Bayreuth. They were said to be engaged, but this affair, too, came to an end, and so abruptly that Hitler left the house with his staff at an hour's notice and took up his headquarters in a little town near Bayreuth.

His romance with his niece Angela Raubal, his step-sister Angela's daughter, came to a tragic end. This fair, handsome country girl adored her interesting uncle, and in 1928-1929, his party friends reported that he never went anywhere without her. He called her Geli, she called him Alf. Then there were scenes, she called him a *graulicher Kerl* (a ghastly creature), he called her still worse. In the fall of 1931, she wanted to leave his apartment in the *Braune Haus* in Munich; he refused to let her go and they had a violent altercation at the window of the *Braune Haus*. He started for Hamburg, forbidding her to leave. Alone in the house she began a letter in a perfectly quiet tone. The next morning, September 18, 1931, she was found shot in her room. She was twenty-three.

For quite a few days after the girl's sudden death, Hitler's friends were afraid he would commit suicide, too. Two days after the shooting she was cremated at the Zentralfriedhof in Vienna in the absence of a Roman Catholic priest. Catholic priests do not officiate at the funerals of suicides.

A week later, with the permission of the Austrian Government, Hitler visited her grave, returning the same night. Very dark versions of the story of her death are current in the Party.

Today, eight years later, there lies in her grave only a paper bearing a few words.

Like most uneducated people, Hitler always reads the newspapers, but never a book.

Kaiser Wilhelm, who was no reader in all conscience, was a walking encyclopedia, compared to his successors. For Hindenburg himself stated that he had never read a book on any subject except military affairs since he left the Military Academy, while Hitler, when asked which book had influenced him most, said: "That is a thing that cannot be proved by titles."

In all the six hundred pages of his own book, there is not a single quotation from a German author; he knows none. Since he speaks no foreign language, everything has to be translated for him. He knows nothing about sports, can neither ride a horse nor drive a car. His favorite exercise is walking, but he always take a hippo-hide whip with him, just in case. He never sees the people now, since he is surrounded by uniformed men on all visits, while several rows of troops cut him off from the crowd on his processions.

I was once able to observe the actor in him. In 1931, I was talking to some American journalists in the lounge of the Kaiserhof in Berlin, when they drew my attention to Hitler, the great party leader. Clad in a brand new overcoat, he was ambling lazily down the wide staircase, playing with the metal rod attached to hotel keys to make guests remember to hand them over to the porter before leaving. He was whirling the key round on the rod, to his own great amusement. Suddenly, about 20 paces off, he became aware of our group. That very second he dropped his hand to his side, stiffened his arms and legs, put on an expression of gloom, and, for our benefit, was transformed into Napoleon. Moved to the depths by his own schemes, he strode slowly past us.

His vanity is so great that he lives surrounded by his own portraits. His friend Troost once made him a carved wooden chest to keep his papers in. In the course of the work he asked Hitler what he should put in the large space left free in the middle of the lid. Hitler at once replied: "That's where my picture goes in profile." On one occasion, he bought up at once a picture of himself as Lohengrin. His speeches are so punctuated with "I's" one gets the impression that Hitler regards world history as material for his own biography. Plunging into his speeches as if into a delicious bath, he is reluctant to quit them, and has delivered public speeches for as long as three and a half hours without growing tired. When he delivered his first speech as Chancellor, on February 6 or 8, 1933, we were on a visit to President Masaryk at his country house near Prague, and had all assembled around the radio in the hall to listen in. The President, then 83 years of age, perhaps the most cultured European of his time, and unquestionably the most distinguished ruler, listened with bent head. Then Masaryk rose, retired without a word, appeared half an hour late the next morning and said: "Forgive me. I could not sleep. And that is the Germany of Goethe and Kant!"

With his insatiable desire to fascinate everybody, an individual judgment of this kind would infuriate Hitler if it ever came to his ears. On one side of the frontier he rules over eighty million people. On the other side, there are fifty or a hundred journalists writing against him. That is a fact he cannot stomach, and he is the only head of State who thunders against the hostile press abroad in every speech. Natures born to rule want power; Hitler does not. Hitler wants what actors want—continuous applause, and applause, moreover, from every living being. He is not proud enough to live with visions of new conditions and new lands, despising his enemies, like Napoleon, hating them like Bismarck, or even forgetting them like Caesar. He dreams of the ceaseless cries and jubilations of a crowd which, in his mind's eye, has swelled from hundreds to thousands, from thousands to millions, in the end spanning the earth. Alienists are familiar with the mania which drives a man to drown the memory of a defeat or insult suffered as a youth in gigantic self-aggrandizement. Not Bismarck, not Frederick the Great, but Napoleon is the ideal of this frenzied German. When my book on Napoleon appeared some twelve years ago, he read it three times, marking it with huge red strokes in the margin, as his now-murdered friend Strasser told me in 1926. (Some émigrés even accuse me in jest of having started the whole thing.) His great dream is to outdo Napoleon. He forgets only one thing, that Napoleon was superior to all men living in one point: he was the greatest soldier and military commander of his time, while Hitler could not even work a machine gun.

He is, however, a greater orator, and has to prove it ceaselessly. That is why he sets out on one of his huge propaganda campaigns through Germany every year. The rush by air from town to town, the ranks of soldiers presenting arms, the cheering crowds, the brilliantly lighted halls, the floodlights and loud-speakers all mean to him what the thunder of the big guns meant to a soldier of olden times. Then he is the great commander, affirming his power by talking. Then his torturing resentment against the artist he could not be is soothed, and he decrees the construction of the biggest hall in the world, the widest motor road in the world, the fastest airplanes in the world.

Frenzied natures of this kind are subject to sudden relapses into depression or brutality. We are told by Goebbels that the very man who, on June 30, 1934, slapped his own friends, standing defenseless before him, suddenly burst into tears when he was appointed Chancellor.

Hitler, oscillating between savagery and melancholy, dreads the castles and palaces he builds for himself, and lives like a retired tradesman in a country house, hung with the pictures retired tradesmen love—those of Grützner, for instance, with jovial monks brandishing glasses of wine, or *Sin*, by Stuck, in which a sinister beauty, bathed in greenish light, is held in the coils of a snake. Then again he will sit in a Munich café with his friends for three hours at a time, consuming quantities of whipped cream and apple tart. Or he will suddenly conceive of a new building scheme, and if one of his ministers ventures to mention expense, he retorts in a rage that he cannot be bothered with details. No genius of action has ever neglected details. Napoleon once inquired of his minister why the price of salt in Marseilles had increased by a penny.

For that matter, nobody is allowed to contradict him. Should anyone make the attempt, Hitler strides to the window, beats a tattoo on the pane with his fingertips and waits until the official has left. Nobody but a lunatic would say to the British Ambassador, three days before the outbreak of war: "I would sooner make war at fifty than at fifty-five," or: "I am an artist and wish to retire from politics altogether." In the first published reports by the British Ambassador, Henderson, Hitler is shown as a man mentally unbalanced, with the government as dependent on his moods as though Germany were an Oriental sultanate with viziers who bowed before their lord, not knowing whether he had been charmed or annoyed by a slave girl in the night, and hence was well or ill-disposed.

In moments of excitement, he will issue from his somber brooding and launch a sudden decision like a thunderbolt. Then nothing is too much for him. He will command, consult, fly, dictate for twenty-four hours on end, without sleep, without meals. For a few days he makes world history. After a week of extreme strain of the kind, he will retire just as suddenly, become invisible, and go tramping in the woods of his mountain home accompanied by his dog and his hide whip.

VI

War was inevitable. I have repeated that fact publicly for the last five years. It was inevitable because it was not a question of raw materials or colonies, on which two sides can always come to terms. The conflict today is one of two philosophies. History shows that rulers can often reach an agreement at the last moment on material questions, but that moral and philosophical ones have always been decided by war in the end. Hence the frequent wars of religion. We are faced with the paradox that material disputes can be settled peaceably, while differences of ideas are settled mainly by gunfire.

Germany is not the only nation, Hitler only one of many statesmen to have broken treaties, undermined morality, subjected peoples, even in our own day. But he is the first to make amorality a principle and perfidy a religion. Not only does law as the basis of national life come to an end with him, but even the desire for it.

Hitler makes his officers and men confess to a pagan creed which was that of the Germanic tribes two thousand years ago, when Germany was menaced by wolves, and not by S. A. men, and intimidated by bears, and not by the Gestapo. The only difference is that the ancient Germans were forced to kill the animals with spears. A religion suited to men clad in skins and living in dense primeval forests is to be reimposed on a highly industrialized people armed with automatic guns, tanks and poison gas. Most of it can be found in Wagner's operas. It is not by chance that Hitler is a passionate Wagnerian.

This new philosophy aims to force Pangermanism on the world. Hence this war, unlike the last one, is a Crusade, although, like the old Crusades, it has its material motives and consequences too. What is at stake is not a redistribution of corn and oil, but the foundation of a new society. Four hundred years ago, the world united to beat the Turks; it has reunited today, but today it is a much more complex and intricate world.

That is why war was declared against an individual. The guilt of the German people in the matter cannot be denied, for they did not inherit this man, but repeatedly elected him; and even though millions of them did so under compulsion, still more millions worshipped him, and the intellectual leaders of the country were at once on his side. Only a handful of writers and artists resolutely opposed him from the very first day. They are now beyond the German frontiers. It was an honor for the present writer to have his books burned in the great public burning of May 1933.

The severance of intellect and government which has distinguished Germany from all other civilized countries for the last four hundred years, has resulted in the fact that two Germanies have lived before the astonished eyes of the world. The German intellect, which alone has made the name of Germany great, Goethe, Kant and the galaxy of German musicians, everything which serves humanity and has given the Germans their honored place among the nations, has been without influence on the State, and for the most part, has come into being in spite of it. While Prussia, in the course of three hundred years, was developing into a Great Power, culture and art was increasingly alienated from it. Prussia has produced no great musician or artist, and only one great writer, at most. All the rest came from the South, flourished at the little courts or in the Free Cities, and rejoiced in being free from all responsibility of government. Every man who has ever brought glory to the name of Germany in the eyes of the world was born outside of Prussia, in Swabia, Saxony, Austria, the Rhineland or the Hansa cities, or was of mixed birth: Kepler and Gutenberg, Dürer and Holbein, Goethe and Schiller, the Humboldts and the Brentanos, Bach and Handel, Mozart and Beethoven, Haydn and Gluck, Schubert and Weber, Schumann and Wagner, Brahms and Bruckner. The only great minds produced by Prussia, Kant and Lessing, were passionately hostile to the Prussian spirit.

Since the Germans have never known freedom, the best minds abandoned the government to a small, narrow-minded and self-seeking caste. But since that caste represented all that was brilliant in the State, there arose even among the intellectuals a desire to curry favor with it in the hope of a decoration or a title. In the same way, the middle class, dazzled by the brittle splendor of the aristocracy, became reconciled to its domination. Only a few have ever desired to see the powers of the ruling caste under control, to live in freedom. Germany is the country which has never actually had a revolution, not even in 1848 or in 1918. All that happened in 1918 was the snapping of a rusty chain, with the flight of twenty-two German princes and the helpless citizens left behind were forced to liquidate a war they had not begun.

It can be no surprise that a warlike people, after such a defeat, should conceive the desire of rising again and taking its revenge. If things had been different, if that people had ever had any kind of political training, it could have found itself again in the tribute paid soon after the war, by a world so recently hostile, to all its great inventors and scholars, artists and writers.

But the honor of Germany does not reside in the spirit. Not until the Sword again flashes from the ash tree trunk does the wounded honor of the Germans feel itself restored.

The Mirror Hall of Versailles, where history is reflected, had been made the property of the German nation when Bismarck founded the Reich. Now it had become the symbol of German defeat. It was very understandable, but very unwise of Clemenceau to transfer to that hall the scene of the conclusion of peace. Since then, millions of Hitler youths have been inflamed with the idea of standing there once again to dictate peace terms to France as in 1871.

Today the world realizes the warning we gave in vain, that the deepest desire of millions of hearts leads to Paris and nowhere else. On the Rhine, and west of the Rhine, are focused all German songs and poems, all German sagas and legends.

The gulf between the Prussian and the non-Prussian spirit can only be bridged by a partition of Germany into North and South, the South, of course, to include Austria. With this argument, it will be easier to win over the minds of the South, even in Germany. Prussia, like the dictator it was, was always feared and never loved. Hitler, the Austrian, had to disguise himself as a Prussian and adopt the bullying voice and intonation he did not naturally possess in order to make himself feared. And yet even this almighty dictator has not succeeded in welding the Reich into a whole, so great and so deep are sectional prejudices. The particularism for which the Germans have always been condemned is the source of their great achievements. Goethe declared that German culture was possible only because there was not one capital, but half a dozen. If Germany is restored to that condition, its spirit will be fostered and its lust for power neutralized, while as a whole it can run no risk, since the constituent parts will in any case be merged in the European United States to which the war will lead.

Thus the causes of the war will be directly reflected in its results. No people can be inoculated with the desire for freedom by a defeat. It will take a century to wean them from their mania for obedience. Yet the most precious things they have always possessed can be released from bondage and set free. The unity of Germany which endured for the twenty years of Bismarck's peace policy was first strengthened by the Kaiser's imperialism, then shaken by its defeat, while in 1923 it nearly collapsed. Then the passion for revenge helped to promote unity of feeling for ten years. Since his first flare-up, Hitler has shaken the desire for unity to its very depths; it is now weaker than it has ever been since 1870.

As regards the material reasons for a German defeat, others have drawn their conclusions from economic knowledge which I do not possess. I can only point out the inner causes.

In my opinion, the defeat of Germany can be deduced from the following four psychological factors of surprise and disillusionment:

(1) They have been in a state of nervous tension for seven years, and are therefore tired; the other side is fresh.

(2) For the last 125 years, the Germans have never seen an enemy in their country for one moment, hence they have never seen the devastation of war and will flinch in horror.

(3) The long years of weakness and yielding on the part of the democracies has created in their minds a picture of decadence in England and France, whose sudden power will take them by surprise.

(4) The glamor of their Führer, marching from victory to victory for seven years, will vanish at the first defeat, so that, derelict and defrauded, they will revolt inside the country and surrender outside.

These four inner factors will demoralize the Germans sooner than the blockade, to which they are accustomed, and will paralyze their energy, while a free, critical, unexhausted people like the French passed through the ordeal of invasion in the World War, bore every loss and conquered in the end.

Two: MUSSOLINI

Two: MUSSOLINI

IF TWO MEN ATTEND THE OPERA, ONE SITTING IN THE first row of boxes and the other in the gallery, their impressions will be as different as those of a man observing his own time from those of a man studying history. Both have their advantages, the man below hears Caruso's voice without interference, hears his breathing, sees the play of his features and hence learns more about the hero than the other; but the other sees the entire drama unfolding on the stage. Hence, at the great spectacle whose audience we have been for the last twenty-five years, I have reserved two seats, one down below, the other in the gallery, and change seats frequently in the course of a single act.

The comprehension of our own epoch is made easier for us by the fact that we see the actors moving before our very eyes. It is made more difficult because we have no access to their private papers. Without the story of his marriage and his letters to his friends, it would be far more difficult for us to fathom Lincoln's character; documents help us to a better understanding of his public actions. Without the memoirs of Napoleon's court we should have no clearly outlined picture of him. But such sources are closed to us in the case of the living. When I began my study of Roosevelt, I said to him: "The trouble is, Mr. President, that you are still living," to which he replied, laughing: "I can't help it."

Unfortunately, while the whole course of history reveals that personalities are infinitely more interesting than cold statistics and political frontiers, the leaders of one's own time can only be analyzed from their physical make-up and conversation, as a result of the lack of love letters and other intimate documents. At all times, the more intimate material has fascinated contemporaries most, not only out of morbid curiosity, but because great statesmen are more interesting for their motivations than for their effects. For effects perish; of the great empires from Alexander to Napoleon, nothing has survived, but the names, the looks, the anecdotes about the lives of the conquerors have been spread throughout the whole world, to form a treasure house of precepts and models in the hearts of the young.

Even among nations, a remote people is interesting only for its character. What American could become excited about the partition of Poland under some king or other? And with the exception of a few hundred officers, who on the other side of the Atlantic is concerned about marching routes and flying squadrons in the latest conquest of Poland? But the message of the commandant of Warsaw refusing to surrender the city is graven in the heart of every child because an immortal human passion, pride, is revealed in it. That is precisely why the interest of the whole world is concentrated on the figures of the handful of men who determine the history of today. Only the stupid despise a leader because he represents a doctrine they dislike or hate. If I, as a resolute opponent of fascism, had refused to approach the dictators, I should lack the most solid basis for comprehending their motives, and hence should be unable to foresee what their future action will be. Since I have done nothing for the last thirty years but study at first hand the human heart, the characters of nations and their leaders, I have been able to predict in books and lectures the main outline of the events of the last few months for seven years past, and find today only trifling errors of detail.

Mussolini, whom I approached as long ago as 1928, did not seem to me the hated leader of an anti-democratic world. I discovered in him a statesman who might be more —or perhaps less—than we, his political opponents, assumed. Today, eleven years after I parted formally from him, although he has since become the overt friend of Hitler, and the covert enemy of the three great democracies, I have no hesitation in declaring him to be the most interesting statesman I have met in Europe.

In the usual analysis of a human being we begin with what strikes us first and immediately,—with the face. At the first glance at Mussolini's face, we are at once struck with his superiority over most of his allies and opponents. It is certainly necessary to follow the development of that face, an easy matter in view of the host of reproductions. We have only one picture of him in his youth. An intimate friend of his once told me how much he suffered as a young man from being unable to afford having photographs taken. That is probably the psychological reason why he cannot stop having himself photographed today. I saw him studying several photographs attentively before publication, showing both him and myself at his desk, and I at once recognized one of his weaknesses. (But then Hindenburg, too, carefully selected all the photographs he allowed to be published, and he was eighty and should have had the wisdom of age.) Mussolini is so aware of the effect of personal appearance on the crowd, that he would assuredly exchange a victory in battle for the head of hair he lacks. His baldness made Caesar an addict of laurel wreaths, but such a head covering would look a bit too ridiculous today.

The picture of Mussolini at twenty has the glowing eyes of a fanatic, of a poet. Even at that age, he had a busy life behind him. "My real biography," he once said to me, "is contained in the first fifteen years of my life." As a boy, this son of a revolutionary blacksmith in an obscure corner in Italy would sit in the corner when his father's friends came during the winter evenings, and spiced their negus with cinnamon and cloves as if the spirit of insurrection could be strengthened that way. Then the boy saw his admired father wander into prison for inflammatory speeches. At that age he heard how another anarchist threw a bomb at the King of Italy's carriage. In those early years the smithy helped to form his imagination. "Such impressions," he said to me, when talking of his youth, "remain deep in a man. The anvil and the fire inspire one with a passion for the material you would like to fashion to your will." When his father died, thousands of workers followed the hearse. The boy was deeply impressed. "The fact that I came from the people," he told me, "has been my greatest strength all my life." Mussolini had obviously inherited the violent trait in his character from his father and his circle.

But there was his mother, a poor teacher, thoughtful and sensitive, who gave the boy, by heredity and training, the other half of his nature, by which his dark violence was tempered. Neither parent taught him Christianity. It is alien to all Socialist circles, and is particularly powerless in that Italian province which has produced most of Italy's men of violence and dictators,—the Romagna, in which Mussolini was born. But he studied the poets, Shakespeare and Nietzsche, and read D'Annunzio, fifteen years his senior, with passion. And above all—history. His father used to read Machiavelli aloud by the smithy fire to his friends and the boys. That is not a legend. Mussolini told me so himself. But these earliest years formed in his mind an ideal picture of Caesar which he never lost, which he has always struggled to fulfill, and which he has never even distantly approached.

What can become of such a youth, who hardly knows whether he desires the good of the community or his own, whether his aim is the happiness of his people, or power for himself? What is to become of him, with his utter poverty and, more important, the utter contempt for money which even today distinguishes him from many of his own collaborators? He can take to writing. Mussolini began to write at seventeen, and not only articles but social dramas as well. But since no publisher would buy his literary efforts, he struggled along for three years as a teacher and a bricklayer, always surrounded, of course, by Socialists. For his pride could never forget that he had been humiliated in his youth because of his poverty. He went to Switzerland because he was under suspicion as his father's son. At Orbe, he worked twelve hours a day in the chocolate factory; at Lausanne, he carried bricks two stories high 120 times a day and slept under a bridge when he was out of work. At this time, he is said to have always carried a medallion with a picture of Karl Marx on it.

One evening, he saw a family quietly eating a rich dinner in a hotel garden on Lake Geneva, while he was starving. On the point of begging for bread, he was horrified at himself and ran away, although he had not a cent in his pocket. "I have given up all my memories and even the ideal," he wrote at the time in a moving letter to a friend.

"Hunger is a good teacher," he said to me, staring grimly ahead at the mere recollection. "Nearly as good as enemies. What a future was open to me as a Socialist or Communist! And prison is a good school, prison and the sea. At sea one learns patience." Then he enumerated the eleven prisons he had been committed to in four countries, calling them good recreation spots he could not have otherwise afforded.

This erratic existence first began to change to a more settled one after his expulsion from Switzerland. At the age of twenty-one, he became a soldier and a professional journalist. He learned much from both fields of endeavor. His military service he regarded as a training for the future, a training which today may often aid to warn him not to hurry into war. It is strange how most great revolutionaries, opposed to the prevailing system, have turned their time of military service to their own inner purposes. That a rebellious spirit can carry arms, even though they be the arms of a government he opposes, inspires every one of them in youth, and they do not forget it when they are themselves in a position to command. Later, in the World War he did his part as a soldier of over thirty, was wounded, and was soon able to return and write instead of shooting. When he was being operated on after his wound, he is said to have refused an anesthetic in order to look on.

Mussolini however, unlike Hitler, has never maintained that he learned strategy as a private soldier, and once when

I asked him what he would do if a stupid general were to ruin all his work in a war, he burst into his low, wicked laugh, pointed to the floor, and said, "then we all collapse together!" That answer showed me the cynicism with which he regards the future today. For the dictators are all great gamblers: That is even the secret of the charm they have for their people, particularly the women.

Between the ages of twenty and thirty Mussolini did nothing but write. He wrote an enthusiastic biography of Huss, the Czech revolutionary who was burned to death at the Council of Trent. He also wrote a novel of modern times which he delivered in instalments to a local rag because the readers were waiting to know what was going to happen to the hero and his girl. During the whole of this time, however, he never ceased to learn: Europe, statistics, literature, and did his best work in a daily radical Socialist newspaper column, which brought him a circle of personal adherents.

Once when I asked him why he, as a great journalist, gagged the journalists of his own country, he took cover behind the pretext that with the freedom of the press they wrote only what the powerful industrialists and the banks, who owned the papers, wanted to have published. For not even he dares to declare publicly that he is determined to keep the mind of his country under control in order to reach his goal. Once I quoted to him a fine saying by an eminent opponent of his, Professor Borghese, now in exile in Chicago (without, however, mentioning his name):

"What good are all these fine new streets and bridges to me if I can't think as I like on them?"

Then he looked at me with a sly, crafty smile and replied:

"He can think whatever he likes on my bridges."

He is, however, very much attached to his own paper, calls it his favorite child, tells how he himself interviewed great statesmen like Briand just before his own accession to power, and studied their faces; or how he reads everything today, and especially the attacks made on him, and how he thinks to himself now and then: "The ass might have written that better."

II

Together with D'Annunzio, Mussolini brought Italy into the World War in 1915. And yet in August 1914 he was such a complete Socialist that he wrote in his newspaper, "Down with war! We shall remain neutral!" He very soon realized, however, that an ambitious politician, revolutionary or conservative, has more opportunities in war than in peace, that to make his career he seeks war, and welcomes it if it is begun by somebody else. The man whose career is already made tends to eschew war, and keeps neutral in a war begun by somebody else. The great profit every neutral can make out of a war—in power, if he is head of a government, in money if he is a business man—restrains them all from entering into other people's wars.

Mussolini, with whom I had more than one conversation

on these questions, which have again become burning, put forward other motives, and summed up his opinion on the whole matter by saying that Italy, "whoever was the victor, would have been faced at the end of the war by a coalition which would have treated us with contempt irrespective of our alliances. We had to reckon with the possibility of having to stand alone against a number of States, even though they were exhausted. What I wanted first and foremost was the renascence of Italy."

By that, of course, he meant not Italy, but himself. It is no wonder that all upstarts from Caesar to Napoleon have always spoken of their solicitude for their people when they sought to develop and maintain only their own power. Such lies are not always misrepresentations; they are frequently auto-suggestive. What great actor does not believe that given the leading role at the largest theater, he could enact the hero's role better than anyone else and bring audiences of thousands to the box-office? In Italy, however, a Socialist could become leader of the State only as a result of war or revolution. Mussolini calculated that he could turn the one into the other. He staked his political future on victory, for he knew that Germany would be far more sensitive to the hostility of Italy than England would have been. England could at that time and can still conquer a country which consists almost entirely of coastline more quickly than Germany, whose ally, Austria, touched the sea at only one small point.

Mussolini's betrayal of his socialistic doctrine in order

to legitimize his personal power in a belligerent Italy is not excused by the fact that he had been given an example of lack of principle by a dozen of the greater rulers. It shows how little value is attached by most heads of states to the ideas they pretend to be fighting for. As their complacency and self-confidence increase, occasionally to the point of megalomania, the role of leader conferred on them by fate takes precedence over all dogma. No man in a commanding position finds any difficulty in justifying himself in his own eyes if he changes his policy. Even Lenin said: "Revolutions are made with the slogans of the day."

Nor must we forget that the Socialists of every country abandoned their long-cherished political tenets at the outbreak of war in 1914. As true Socialists, their dogma precluded their participation in a capitalistic war, and yet, as a political party, they voted in favor of war credits and took up arms themselves, with a few rare exceptions such as MacDonald in England and Liebknecht in Germany. When Mussolini saw his Socialist comrades engaged in shooting each other—comrades with whom he had been on the best of terms at international congresses so short a time ago, he accepted their war fever as a convenient excuse for involving his own country in the shooting.

It was more difficult for Mussolini to make a revolution after the war than he had at first believed. He was aided, he found, by the "menace of communism." For since he led where Hitler followed, he was the first to summon up the Bogey of Bolshevism. When communistic tendencies first began to appear in Italy after the war, Mussolini employed them as a pretext for hailing himself as the savior of order. But since it took him three years to develop his party army into an effective fighting body, he came too late with his revolution. For when he marched on Rome in October 1922, alleging that he had come to save the nation, in other words to get the power into his own hands, the danger of communism was a thing of the past. But after all, he couldn't very well waste a successful revolution.

He has been reproached with making the "march on Rome" in a sleeping car. That is the modern form of the *coup d'état*. Officers no longer gallop into battle at the head of their troops to wrest the colors from the enemy standard-bearers. Nor do armies join in battle to the stirring tunes of their regimental bands. Mussolini issued his orders from his office in Milan. He actually issued orders, although to all appearances he was merely the editor of a newspaper. And Rome trembled, for it had a Prime Minister whose personal insignificance I had seen with my own eyes a few months before at the Genoa Conference. It is undoubtedly true that the men Mussolini set out to overthrow were weaker than he. That is no proof of the rightness of his idea, but only of the strength of his personality.

A short time before, when on a visit in Berlin, he answered a friend's question about the distribution of power in Italy: "At the moment there are only two powers—myself and the King." This self-confidence represents in him, as it does in most strong natures, half his success. Strangely enough, self-confidence is more productive of success in young men before they have made their way than in older men whose way is already made. In youth it is a pillar of flame lighting the way ahead, later it becomes a part of the furniture, as it were, an altar bearing a steady flame. The greatest danger for the dictator is not an excess of self-confidence before the victory—but megalomania after it. Augustus is the warning example. Caesar was murdered just in time to remain a splendid figure.

How natural Mussolini was, and still is when one is alone with him, I can show by two illustrations. In October 1922, the King, surrounded by his weaklings, yielded to the advancing army of the revolutionary Fascists and summoned their leader to the head of government by telegraph. Mussolini received the momentous telegram in his editor's office. He flung open the door to the next room where his brother was supervising the printing of the paper.

"Arnoldo," he shouted, "get the stop-press ready."

"What for?"

"My appointment!"

And he closed the door and went back to work on the article he had been writing.

Another time I saw him in the reverse situation. Each

afternoon, during the time we were carrying on the conversations I had prepared, alone together in the vast hall of the Palazzo Venezia, he was utterly natural. Once, however, when a man came to repair the telephone, he was unnatural with me because he was playing up to the workman, who he knew would later tell his mates what the Duce was really like. Only people prone to pose themselves have described him as a poseur.

On the other hand, if he is speaking on the Piazza, or appearing at great parades, he adopts, whether on horseback or in his car, the pose the people love. For just as Americans would laugh at a President who drove through the streets, his brow dark with care, the Italians expect that attitude in the head of their State. The emotionalism of the Italians is one of the few reasons why dictatorship has survived so long in Italy.

This naturalness was the sole instrument by which Mussolini, who came to power at the age of 40, has kept it for seventeen years. Instead of roaring and attitudinizing, Mussolini, immediately upon seizing power, began to adopt that pliancy toward persons and parties which has at all times been the distinguishing mark of the diplomacy of his country.

Mussolini was not the first dictator in Italy; there had been, as he told me himself, nine hundred before him. (He seems to have included every bullying burgomaster in his sum total.) But none of them, not excepting Caesar Borgia and the other great condottieri whom Mussolini resembles physically and mentally, was in any way a wild, barbaric soldier. The training of centuries at the courts of Popes, Dukes and great city states had developed leaders for this Mediterranean people who combined elegance with boldness, ruthlessness with skill. No present-day people possesses men such as these, and there were none before them who combined these qualities except the tyrants of Sicily.

By virtue of this astuteness, craft and adroitness, Mussolini managed to veil his revolution so well that, as he expressed it himself, he began with a 50% revolution, let the rival parties exist for years, and then slowly suppressed them. Yet he had one outstanding man murdered. When I mentioned the name of Matteoti, which had probably never been pronounced all these years in his room, he replied with perfect calm: "Political crimes are just as frequent in the democratic states. Under Napoleon III and in the French Republic there were plenty of mysterious cases, and there have been more murders in the new Germany [1932] than in any other country."

If we compare with this the brutal haste with which Hitler, within three months, disarmed every other party by murder and imprisonment, we realize again the gulf which lies between the skillful Southerner and the raging barbarian of the North.

Mussolini is remarkable for the swift resolution with which he comes to his really great decisions. When I asked him once what he would have done if his march on Rome had been a failure, he cried:

"I never thought of it. If I had thought that failure was possible, how could I have acted?" He uttered these words with a sharp hostile note of finality, almost like a general remembering his greatest victory. At such moments his voice, his look, the quick, rare movements of his right hand make him the very embodiment of the man of will. Such mannerisms are rare in the composed, steady and unemotional answers of the man; they betray a lifetime of self-command. He told me how he had written his first political essay, thirty years before, on "The Virtue of Patience" because he possessed too little of it himself.

III

The only segment of a dictator's activity completely exposed to the world is his foreign policy. His greatest internal struggles, his relations with his officials, all that he must do, day by day and hour by hour, to prevent his friends from turning into enemies, is known only through occasional scraps of information. The tensions and passions among the leading Fascists, the hatred with which one of the most famous pursues his former friend and chief, are known far beyond Rome itself. Such passions have flourished at all times in the courts of caliphs and emperors and the tents of triumvirs, and have often led to the assassination of men who have risen too far above others.

Such men, of course, compare themselves with their great prototypes. Mussolini regards Napoleon with a very critical eye. Like Kemal Pasha, the late founder of modern Turkey, he expatiated in detail upon all of Napoleon's mistakes, and what he, Mussolini, intended to do to avoid them. "Perhaps there was something brutal about him," he said to me, speaking of Napoleon, and seemed quite unaware of the fact that he, too, had many such impulses. "For that matter, the Jacobins were against him because he had throttled the Revolution, the Legitimists because he was an upstart, the clergy on account of the Pope. Only the mob loved him: under him they had food. Besides, the mob has most feeling for glory. For glory cannot be grasped logically; it is a matter of sentiment. All the same, my respect for him has increased in the last few years."

When I asked him whether he felt like Bonaparte in his youth, who said that an empty throne incited him to sit on it, Mussolini made his ironic face, opening his eyes wide but at the same time smiling quite broadly, and said: "Thrones have lost considerably in glamor since then."

For Caesar, and for him alone, Mussolini has a truly religious veneration. Once I attempted to warn him against his flatterers, one of whom had just left the room. I reminded him of the fool whom Caesar had kept secreted in his chariot to warn him against the jubilation of the populace. He turned very grave, nodded and said he knew that danger intimately. Caesar, however—! "Caesar's murder was a disaster for mankind." Then he added in a low, but strangely agitated voice:

"I love Caesar. The greatest of all men who have ever

lived. They wanted to bring him the head of his friend Pompey; instead, Caesar prepared solemn burial for him. He is the only man ever to have united the strength of will of the soldier with the genius of the sage. He was at bottom a philosopher who saw everything from the point of view of eternity. He loved glory, it is true, but his ambition did not estrange him from humanity."

Another time, when I had again brought the conversation around to Caesar, he turned round, picked up a book lying open on a table behind him, and read a few lines in Italian from the opening scene of Shakespeare's *Julius Caesar*. Then he slowly replaced the book, leaned on his elbow, and made one of the pauses he seems to require during his philosophic conversations, although not in his histrionic speeches.

"And yet," he said at last, "it is incredible that he fell into the trap." I asked him whether he meant the historical one. "Of course. Didn't he know all the ruses of conspirators? Most likely he did not know what to do next, and sought death himself."

This strange interpretation of Caesar, and in a general way his love for him, are both part and parcel of Mussolini's contempt for the mass of the people, a contempt which, moreover, he shares with Caesar. He discussed these matters much more sincerely than others, with me at any rate, and I developed a great deal of historical perspective from those conversations. In any case, he believes that nobody can rule without first making himself feared.

"Even a dictator can be loved," he said to me another time, "provided that the mob has a healthy fear of him, too. The mob loves strong men. The mob is a female."

From this standpoint, we can understand the hate-love which all dictators feel towards the mob. I once found the Duce in uniform in his room because he was expecting a Fascist demonstration below and wished to greet it. I was afraid he would strike a new attitude. The staircase of the huge palace was crowded with officers, in loud, laughing mood, and I felt out of place as the only civilian. But inside his room, Mussolini was perfectly composed, and showed no trace of the actor's nervousness. He questioned me about Abyssinia (this was long before the war, of course) and I told him something of the sources of the Blue Nile. When the cries of the populace called him to the balcony, I went to the next window and observed his profile as he looked down on the stormy sea of the shouting crowd with a patriarchal, ironic expression. Then he held up his hand for silence, spoke some thirty sentences which said nothing, received another ovation, came back and asked me to go on at the point at which we had been interrupted.

He uttered not one critical word of the crowd. But the way he passed over the incident as an interlude, without referring to it, the sight of his profile, the emptiness of the phrases he had flung to the crowd, showed me the depth of his contempt.

"The mass," he said later in reply to my question, "means

as much to me as a herd of sheep until it is organized. I have nothing against it. I merely deny that it can govern itself. Whoever leads it must do so by a double bridle: enthusiasm and interest, the mystical and the political side. Can I expect the crowd to lead the thorny, dangerous life I lead? That is for the few. Every speech to the crowd has a double purpose, to throw some light on a situation and to give the masses an idea to chew on. Hence for the provocation of a war public speeches are indispensable. There is always hope for those who cannot be influenced by such speeches. I have known their effects for thirty years. In Milan I could empty the streets when I was announced."

When I returned that, according to his own account, he prepared his own speeches months ahead, so that the sight of the masses could alter nothing, he said:

"It is like the building of an American house. First comes the whole scaffolding, a construction of steel. Then concrete or brick, or even precious material is thrown into it. For my speeches in October, the scaffolding is ready in April. It then depends on the atmosphere in the Piazza, on the eyes and voices of the mob, whether I fill it up with travertine or brick or marble. The crowd doesn't have to know, it must believe. It must submit to being shaped. When I feel the mass in my hands, there comes over me at times a repulsion such as the sculptor feels for the marble, which he sometimes shatters in rage because it cannot per-

fectly body forth his vision. Everything depends on domi-
nating the mass like an artist."

The astonishing thing about it is that the mob does not
notice this contempt. Having studied and loved the Italian
character for years, I believe it to be critical, artistic, emo-
tional, undisciplined and thoroughly unwarlike. Of all
these characteristics, only the emotionalism seems to go
with fascism. Mussolini is perfectly well aware of all this.
That this critical knowledge of his people has never hin-
dered him in the great experiments of his life is either
foolhardy or admirable. For even though he can do without great wars, he cannot do without war-mongering,
tanks, men-of-war and the general militarization of a
nation in no way fitted for it. He admitted to me himself
that it was unprecedented in the history of a critical people
like the Italians that they should be trained to mass-feeling
and collective life. He also frankly admitted that his procedure was exactly the same as Stalin's with the Russians.
Yet here lie the limits to his adventures. This very skepti-
cism towards his own people, his penetrating understanding of their foibles, may one day be his salvation.

IV

In his own articles, as well as in our conversations, there
is nothing that Mussolini has criticized more sharply than
any form of racial theory. That was before Hitler's rise to

power, hence I had absolutely no political motive for hearing what he had to say on the subject.

"Of course there isn't a pure race left," he said with vivacity. "Even the Jews have not remained apart. The strength and beauty of a nation has often been due to its mingling with others. The Americans are the best proof of the advantages of racial intermixture. Race is a feeling, not a reality; 95% is feeling. I shall never believe that the degree of purity of a race can be biologically proved. It is odd that the prophets of the so-called nobility of the German race were none of them Germans; Gobineau was French, H. S. Chamberlain was English, Laponge again French. Chamberlain even went so far as to call Rome the capital of chaos. National pride needs no delirium of race." And when I turned the talk to anti-Semitism, he added:

"We have none in Italy. Jewish Italians have always been good citizens and fought bravely as soldiers. They occupy eminent positions in universities, banks and the army. Quite a number are generals. Della Seta is one of our greatest scholars."

This tolerance goes well with his profoundest feelings about God and fate. When we were speaking of these things on Easter Eve, and he called himself a fatalist, when he told me how, as a boy, he had disliked the organ and candles in the church, and nonetheless had called on God for help in his first speech in the Chamber. I confronted him with the question whether a disciple of Machiavelli could believe in anything.

"In himself. That would be something," he replied quickly, with a smile. Then he bent forward into the circle of the lamplight and went on:

"In my youth I believed in nothing. I had called on God in vain to save my mother. Everything mystic is alien to me, like the colors and sounds of the monastery where I lived for a time as a lad. Not that I exclude the possibility of a supernatural phenomenon once having happened or that Nature is divine. I now believe that there is a divine power in the universe. Men can worship God in many ways, and each must be left to his own." And when I pointed to the dilemma between free will and fate, he made the fine reply:

"We must react with our will against fatalism. It is an interesting struggle. Our wills must prepare the ground upon which our fates are to unfold. To act, to create! What is glory in comparison? At most the consolation that we shall not utterly die. Immortality is the pledge of glory. But it comes—afterwards!"

V

A comparison with Hitler redounds to Mussolini's credit at every point.

Hitler's effect lies in his intonations; to reach his goal he had to be an orator, a great popular orator such as Germany had never known. Even the leading popular parties had not had a great orator for one or two generations.

In Hitler there appeared an orator who fascinated the

Germans because his eloquence was the counterpart of Wagner's music; a relentlessly recurring motif, over-instrumentation, sobs and cries, persuasion, almost intimidation, by massed choirs, and over the whole a kind of musical mist compounded of God, heroes and race, just as in Lohengrin. Hitler's sole musical love is Wagner, who appeals even to the unmusical, and he applies what he learns from him to his speeches, the pompousness coupled with nebulosity, the brutality coupled with innocence—all of which make his speeches so fascinating to the Germans. All in all, Hitler probably imagines the act of government to be like an act of a Wagner opera with glittering stage sets. Mussolini, on the other hand, finds his models in history, not on the stage.

When Mussolini speaks on the Piazza, his metallic voice goes home to the crowd in simple sentences like the blows of a hammer. They go home saying: "We understand him. The man is right." When Hitler speaks, a nebulous mist obscures the hall, he works himself up into a half-screaming bit of weeping. His audience is stirred and goes home saying: "We couldn't understand a word. How great he must be!" Mussolini speaks in a country where nearly every man is a born orator. Hence his eloquence could not impress the crowd; he won it to his side only after much time. The difference between their ways of speaking, clarity and mysticism, tallies exactly with the popular music of the two nations, Verdi and Wagner.

The two dictator-orators are further distinguished by

the fact that the one hardly ever speaks of himself, the other hardly ever of anything else. Even when Mussolini delivered his speech of victory after the Abyssinian war in May 1937, he said "I" only twice. Hitler says it at least a hundred times in every speech. For him, modern German history is an expression of his personality.

Hitler's book is permeated with aggressiveness and hatred. Mussolini, too, can hardly be called a loving soul; he once said to me that he did not belong to the type of Caesar, who forgot and forgave his enemies, but to that of Bismarck, who never ceased to hate them. Yet his action is constructive and he governed Italy for thirteen years without a war.

Mussolini is a thorough man, the father of a big family which he constantly increases. (He is by no means a faithful husband. Three women are known to have been his mistresses, a Russian, a Jewish and a French woman.) When he first began his régime, he drove his car through the whole country to show the people that he could "drive." Now, at 56, he has passed his test as an airplane pilot. From time to time he wields the ax himself or rides on a tractor, to provide a tangible example.

Hitler has a dread of physical exertion; he cannot even drive a car; even in that, his wasted fruitless youth takes its revenge. There is in him, moreover, the feeling of the actor who would like to play the King. While Mussolini's whole appearance today is typically that of a man of the people, Hitler betrays his petty bourgeois origin by the fact that he cannot even choose the proper coat or tie for an occasion. While Mussolini shows in all he does a feeling for stateliness—in his gigantic hall, for instance—Hitler's rooms betray the taste of a paperhanger.

Mussolini, by fifteen years of work, has steadily increased his cultural status. He learned German and French in early life, English only after he had become dictator. Hitler, who learned nothing in the eight years which the young Mussolini spent in preparation, has found no time to learn a single language. Mussolini incessantly teaches himself; Hitler incessantly preaches to others. Every visitor to Mussolini is questioned; when he goes, Mussolini has learned something new. Every visitor to Hitler declares that the megalomaniac had the conversation all to himself. He thunders at his visitor, rolls his eyes, drums on the window pane. Suddenly, the guest finds himself dismissed.

Hitler has time and to spare for a chat; Mussolini never has any. The one leaves his capital only in summer, if at all, works ceaselessly with all his departments, never goes out, never entertains. He works. Hitler spends the best part of the year at his villa in a remote corner of the Reich. And who are his associates there and in Berlin? By choice, film actors.

We are told that both men restored self-respect to their peoples. Strange, indeed, when we consider that free speech is forbidden. But if this muzzling of the spirit were true or not, the fact would be far less dangerous for the world in Italy than in Germany. In the first country, a characteristically critical people had to be trained—perforce—to greater discipline, but Mussolini the cynic knows his people's foibles. Hitler, on the other hand, really believes in the nonsense he utters about the Germanic race. In Germany, the most disciplined people of the earth, instead of being released into freedom, are being lashed into slavery, the most extreme form of obedience. Mussolini was confronted with a people which had for centuries been regarded as unwarlike, and strove in his own way to train it for war.

While Mussolini has had to contend ceaselessly with the notion of freedom inherent in the Italians, all Hitler had to do was to tell the Germans, who had never been free, that their brief excursion into freedom had led them astray. The essence of the State was Authority—and the whole nation was at his feet. It took Mussolini eight years before the last professor took the oath, Hitler, eight weeks. When I said to Mussolini, long before Hitler's rise, that all he lacked was Germans as his material, his eyes sparkled with admiration for the drill system of old Prussia.

VI

The world was all the more amazed when it saw the sane dictator bow to the mad one. And to explain this, there are hidden weaknesses as well as secret reasons.

I first realized the weaknesses when Mussolini revised the conversations of which fragments have been quoted here. After having read the proofs, altered nothing, approved everything, published passages in his press and then released the book for publication in all countries, he was so startled by its effect that he abridged a second edition of the Italian version, deleting everything relating to God, fatalism, the Church and faith. That was due to pressure from the Vatican. All Italy heard about it and compared the two editions.

His manner of yielding on this point, and the details of how it came about showed me how susceptible he was to influence.

Far worse was his conversion to the doctrine of race, which he had always derided. That was Hitler's stipulation for signing a great contract for the delivery of ores and other things which Mussolini direly needed. The delivery was made dependent on that great public *volte-face,* so that Hitler need not stand alone in the world as a racial persecutor. For the same reason, Mussolini suddenly banned the works of Machiavelli, till then his bible, from all schools and universities, for it was Machiavelli who had warned Italy against any alliance with the northern barbarians.

Before concluding with the question of what Mussolini will do in the coming years, let us look back and see what he has done for Italy in the past seventeen.

Abroad, he has subjected a few million black men whose country is reputed to contain fabulous treasures, which have made no appearance so far. The Abyssinian War was piracy without profit. Mussolini has unquestionably increased the world's respect for the power of Italy while reducing its love for Italy's beauty. Before him, the country was greatly loved, now it is *not* greatly feared.

At home he has striven to change the national character, and all lovers of Italy rejoice to see that he has been no more successful than anybody else could have been in so short a time. Order has not increased, the trains are as late as ever. The people of the South, who have an aversion for long hours of work, used to meet on the Piazza at half-past eleven to gossip; they now do so at a quarter to twelve. No class is better off than it was before. And during all this time, intellect and culture have fled the land, and not one poet or artist has arisen to fill the gap they left. The greatest minds of Italy have been banished. Mussolini stands responsible to history for having been the first to suppress freedom in a civilized country and hence encouraged other adventurers to do the same in theirs. The roads and canals, the air and shipping lines, which are the boast of his régime, came into being, not through him, but through the spirit of the age, since the same improvements were carried out at the same time by the great democracies. Nor did he even increase Italian armaments more than those of other countries at the same time.

Of so-called fascism, whose connotations come more and more to mean nothing but concentration, nothing will remain after the death of its leader but a new external relation between capital and labor, a change attempted

in every other country at the same time. The so-called co-
operative state is an empty phrase, created to conceal the
suppression of popular representation. Amid more or less
violent convulsions, to which the royal family may suc-
cumb, the Italian people will return to its true nature and
its honest expression. Whether a Socialist state ever comes
into being in Italy depends on the outcome of the present war.

Thus the only thing he can claim for himself before
the bar of history, after his huge sacrifices of blood and
liberty, is that an interesting and highly-gifted personality
attracted the attention of the world for so long. He has
become an idea; he has revived the romantic notion of the
condottieri of the Renaissance and the dictator of classical
times. Whether he will enter history as a great organizer
or a tragic figure depends on the fifth act of his life, for
Mussolini is faced now with the most pregnant decision
of his career:

Should he enter the war or not?

The only thing in favor of his entry now is that, at the
end of the war, he might find himself as in 1915, faced with
a power or a coalition which might manhandle him badly.
That is probable insofar as the fall of one dictator might
hasten the downfall of the other before the opinion of the
world. Should the state form, not founded but reintro-
duced by Mussolini, collapse in Germany, which is inevitable if Italy remains neutral, people might be moved
to extirpate it altogether. "Neutrals," he once said to me,

"are always repulsive, like a man who tries to get out of a fight."

On the other hand there are important reasons for his remaining neutral, for he will hardly find his way into the Entente. Personally, in culture and knowledge, he is a great friend of the French *esprit* and despises the German. "The misfortune," he once said to me, "was that Varus let himself be beaten by the Germans in the year 9."

A further argument in favor of his remaining neutral is his respect for the English fleet, which, together with the French fleet, could shoot half his coast to pieces, even if his own army were occupying Nice. Further, he is well aware of the passionate antipathy of the whole Italian people, including most convinced Fascists, for Hitler and the Nazis. He also realizes the Italian aversion to war and the gratitude they would feel towards him if he did not lead them into it. Finally, he is threatened with revolution if he does go to war.

Hence, it is quite possible that if Mussolini maintains his so-called benevolent neutrality, Hitler's fall may be accomplished before our eyes while Mussolini, for his part, might free his people from their financial and dietary difficulties with the proceeds of the high price of his neutrality.

Mussolini, who in seventeen years of government has conducted only one mild war against African Negroes, and has always kept out of European wars, is not afflicted with Caesarean delusions. For the most part, what I myself observed holds true only up to 1932. Friends tell me that Mussolini has changed in the last seven years. I do not believe that a man in his fifties, remaining in the same position and power, can change his nature without the stimulus of great new events. He has founded a so-called "Impero," which extends over ten million Negroes, brings nothing in revenue, costs millions for its maintenance, and serves mainly as a source of jokes and anecdotes for his people. He founded his empire with the intention of giving a cheap demonstration of his theory of war, and to find fresh points of support.

Today not a man in Italy calls on him to take up arms against France, for France is much more popular in Italy than Germany. France's last victory was not over Italy, nor has France forced any treaty on Italy. The feeling of revenge, which prevails among the youth of Germany trained by Hitler, is utterly absent from a country which fought the last war side by side with France.

Far from being a matter of compulsion, the decision lies simply and solely in Mussolini's hands. If he plunges into his imitator's adventure, he will perish with him. If he refrains, it will be seen how superior he was to him in statesmanship.

Three: STALIN

Three: STALIN

ON THE BIRTHDAY OF THE CZAR, THE LEADING
personalities of the province, in brilliant uniforms, were
assembled in the Cathedral, standing and kneeling by
turns in intercession for the life of Alexander III. Up in
the gallery, the voices of an invisible boys' choir were
heard, and as the sound died away, the voice of a single
boy was heard, so pure and strong that the congregation
below listened breathlessly, delighting in the gift of the
boy singing above. Nobody except the conductor of the
choir, who had discovered him, knew who he was.

It was in Tiflis, the capital of Georgia. The day was
February 26, 1894, and the boy singing so beautifully in
honor of his beloved Czar was a cobbler's son whose
mother, by a great effort, had entered him in the priests'
seminary so that one at least of the family might rise above
its poverty and take holy orders. Such was the paradoxical
beginning of Josef Stalin's career.

Yet it was precisely the religious training which was forced upon him that inculcated in him that spirit of contradiction and suspicion which drove him to an opposite extreme.

"People say," he told me, "that I became a Socialist by inward conviction at ten or even six years of age. There isn't a bit of truth in it. My parents were utterly uneducated, but they were very good to me. It was in the seminary that I first began to oppose the régime. It was swarming with spies. At nine in the morning we were summoned to our tea, but when we got back at half-past, all our drawers had been searched. And they rummaged in our hearts as they rummaged through our papers. It was disgusting. Then, as a protest, I was ready for anything! And when the first illegal groups of Russian Marxists came into the Caucasus, I at once took to their writings."

In telling such stories, and especially if he has left his pipe at home, he speaks in a low and toneless voice. The boy's rich voice seems to have passed away with all his religious memories. We were sitting at a long conference table in the bare, well-lighted, moderately-sized room in an annex of the Kremlin. As Stalin spoke, he drew sketches and figures for two hours without stopping on sheets of paper which he took from a pile in front of him, and then threw into the waste paper basket when they had fulfilled their enigmatic function. He drew only with red lead, a fact which is particularly interesting because his pencil also contained a blue lead, but which he never used.

It is possible that he draws continually not from rest-
lessness but only in order to avoid looking at his visitor.
I, at any rate, seldom caught a glimpse of that great be-
trayer of the human soul, his eye, which is gray, with a
veiled or at any rate shadowed look.

It was a long road which brought him here, to his power
and solitude, and a far more winding one than the one
which brought me to the moment when I sat beside him.
For him, that room and what it means is the goal of life.
For me, the man was a butterfly I had caught by the way-
side to preserve in my collection of human characters.
In all truth, I cannot say that he is the most interesting
specimen. Yet I reflect with a certain admiration on the
enormous vitality that must have been in the man to bring
him into that room. What a full, adventurous life, what
hundreds of physical dangers, of temptations of the soul,
what thousands of sudden surprises, big and little, disil-
lusions and self-denials, acts of daring and humiliation; a
chain of emotions running through forty years, a life
packed with feeling rather than thought, and with action
rather than feeling!

Monomaniacs of this kind, who in their youth had
glowed for an ideal, who had sacrificed every joy in life
on its altar, are slowly and often unconsciously transformed
into men who seek power for its own sake. But even when
they have attained their power, more than power alone is
their incentive. However often they may forget their boy-
hood's dream, it rises again and again before them. The

real revolutionary, and Stalin is the only genuine one among the three dictators, can never quite lose his first vision. Whoever imagines, when looking at Stalin's amazingly circuitous path in life, that he has renounced revolution, has a surprise in store for him one day.

When the cobbler's son and novice in the Greek Orthodox Church forsook the religious world, he at once set out on his difficult path under a disguise. He had been in the custom of putting on a workman's smock and leaving secretly in order to join his new friends. Once he was recognized on the way home from one of his meetings, and as he had long been under suspicion for reading forbidden literature, he was expelled from the monastery at a day's notice.

What was his name? An unpronounceable heap of Russian syllables which he has even forgotten himself. He first called himself Sosso, then Kobo, David Ivanovitch, and only in his late twenties, by way of other aliases, did he arrive at his self-chosen name of Stalin, which suits him neither mentally nor physically.

For seventeen years he was forced to live anonymously under a series of names as the police were constantly on his track. This illegal life has always been the fate and at the same time the secret delight of subterranean agitators, even in the ancient world. The insecurity of his daily life implants in a young soul distrust of every acquaintance, caution before every friend, and above all, suspicion. With perpetual changes of residence to escape the police, with the everchanging aliases, disguises, beards, his life is one long course of study in dissimulation. It is a rarity to be proclaimed from the housetops, when a man like Stalin either preserves or regains his early simplicity.

Before judging the man of 60 who has risen to be an all-powerful dictator, we must form a clear picture of the early life of the poor artisan's son. It is the only way to understand him.

Stalin, for instance, was from his eighteenth to his thirty-eighth year relentlessly pursued as an agitator, repeatedly banished, always a fugitive, from Tiflis to Batum, from Batum to Baku, from Baku to St. Petersburg. Between his flights from city to city, he was six times in prison, for periods of three to ten months; he was exiled to Siberia, escaping five times at the end of a few weeks or months to reappear under a new name. Between times a bookbinder, a compositor, a printer of prohibited papers in cold cellars, or again a traveling agitator in tobacco factories or coal mines. Can such an early life, with its sacrifices of money and security, of the cheerful, hopeful education of children, of the respect of the world about him, with no hope of reward or fame—can such a life, if it does not break the man who bears it, make him other than a passionate champion of his community and an ever greater fanatic?

Only such a faith can compensate a man who feels the growth of his inward powers, his superiority, his influence on other men, for his lack of worldly possessions. Stalin, too, like many of his comrades, could have chosen a public political career as a deputy in the Opposition or as the editor of a liberal paper. Even there he could oppose the Czar and work for the laborers of Russia. But he preferred, in prison, to write secret messages, to other friends in the same prison, in milk or urine on innocent looking sheets of newspaper. He preferred to plot new revolutionary exploits with them, or, surrounded by armed soldiers, plan a new escape from the icy regions of Irkutsk.

A conspirator's life, always illegal yet never seeking the ringing reward of the equally illegal life of crime, must create a cynical picture of the world in a man's soul. While above this world, in ever remoter spheres, there hovers the vision of a hope whose fulfillment he cannot believe he will see. The character thus formed must differ—radically— not only from that of a politician trained in universities, clubs and parliaments, but also from that represented by Mussolini and Hitler, neither of whom, for all the difference between their early lives, ever needed to hide or to assume strange names and disguises. The tyrant of the country in which he spent his youth has bequeathed to Stalin, in spite of the novelty of some of his ideas, the methods of an Asiatic tyrant, as an example to be emulated.

II

Throughout his early revolutionary work, Stalin remained at the extreme left of the radical wing, contesting everything which had been "Menshevist," that is, of the minority and reform party. The Mensheviks were an off-shoot of the split in the Socialist Party which took place at the Congress of London in 1903, which Stalin attended at the age of 24. Nothing would satisfy him but the radical solution: terror, assassination, insurrection. He had accepted his whole program from a single man who, from the moment he met him, was his sole and unconditional leader. This was Lenin, who had been living abroad for twelve years at that time, and whom Stalin visited during his visits to Cracow and Vienna, and later to Finland, first to receive his instructions, and later to take his orders.

That Stalin is the disciple of Lenin rather than of Marx we can tell by his writings. It is even possible that he loved Lenin. In any case today, when his power far exceeds any that Lenin ever had, Stalin feels that he is the second of a line. When I spoke to him of the succession of Peter the Great, he answered simply: "I am a disciple of Lenin. My only wish is to become a worthy one. If a comparison must be found, the only man to compare with Lenin is Peter the Great. But I, for my part, am merely Lenin's disciple."

Since I have no doubt of the truth of this confession, I can only explain this unusual modesty in a dictator, this voluntary retreat to the second place, by a personal veneration which seems otherwise alien to Stalin's nature and is unique in his life. Such characters do not generally harbor feelings of gratitude.

And gratitude for what? Lenin, I believe, owed more

to his disciple than his disciple owes to Lenin. Lenin, always living and working abroad, found in Stalin the ideal adjutant he would never have had, were Stalin not there. The utter subjection of this man's ambition to his ideals, the non-existence of any shadow of contradiction in twenty years' collaboration, even though much of it went on by letter, are almost without precedent. The blind faith of a man who was, after all, no common employee, but an extraordinarily self-reliant character, was of the greatest advantage for Lenin in gaining his influence over the Russian workers, which was made doubly difficult by Lenin's exile. Stalin was the ambassador of a pretender to the crown, ruling from abroad. During the years of his editorship of the *Pravda*, at that time a small, prohibited sheet in St. Petersburg, he received articles from Lenin and Gorki wrapped in cigarette paper, or recovered them from tins floating in oil casks.

It was Lenin, too, who kept Stalin in Russia. For we can hardly assume that the latter was not from time to time overcome by the wish to spend a few years of study abroad, that is, in freedom and security. When I asked him whether his ignorance of foreign languages caused him any trouble—he speaks none, and has an accent even in Russian, since at home he spoke Georgian—he deprecated the value of other languages.

"Very few of us who lived in Russia," he said, "really remained in as close touch with life here as Lenin did abroad. Every time I went to see him, he had piles of letters from Russian politicians and knew more than those who had remained at home. And yet it was a disaster for him that he had to stay abroad. Today, of the seventy men in the Central Committee, only three or four have lived abroad. But I know many comrades who have spent twenty years in Germany and still cannot give an informative answer to a concrete question."

The radical solution Lenin preached was the result of the defeat of 1905, when the first revolution collapsed under the fire of the Minister Stolypin. Gallows rose for the workers in towns throughout Russia. The gallows were nicknamed, none too pleasantly, "Stolypin's neckties." At that time Lenin fled to Finland, not to see Russia again until its liberation. At the same time, Trotsky was banished to Siberia and Stalin soon followed him.

Since the acts of sheer terrorism committed by the Czar, Lenin permitted and approved of any method of weakening his government, even assassination and robbery. Since the party had no money, and even the marriages of a few secret members to wealthy widows brought in very little, Stalin, in concert with Lenin, who was advising him from abroad, decided on a strong move. One day in June 1907, after careful preparation, they attacked a great bank convoy, which left the capital annually for Tiflis, on the highroad in broad daylight. They killed the cashiers and the clerks in the lorry, and stole the sack of gold which was carried off by a mounted man. Fifty men lost their lives, the perpetrators vanished without leaving a trace behind them. No one was ever brought to trial, but the party was the richer by 341,000 rubles in notes, which later passed unnoticed out of the country.

The story, with all its details, was later recounted in a book by one of the gang in a somewhat bombastic tone. But when I questioned Stalin on the subject, the peasant in him came out. He stood up, fetched a pamphlet containing biographical notes about himself and said, smiling: "You'll find everything about me here."

Such things may have impressed Lenin all the more as he himself could not cooperate in their execution. But he appreciated just as much in Stalin, who was seldom clearly implicated in such crimes, his indefatigable labor among the workers. Stalin, the born adjutant, was the more fitted for such work in that he had not been born in a cultured and wealthy house, but had grown up in the dull round of poverty. When Stalin compared the wretched corrugated iron houses of the oil drillers in Baku with the splendid villas of the oil kings and their directors on the shores of the Black Sea, where I saw them with my own eyes in the same place twenty years later, he must have clenched his fist in his pocket.

Stalin, who repudiates any connection between his revolution and the romantic robbers of the Russian legends, has none the less retained a fond weakness for them; but he speaks of them with the benevolent contempt of a man who really knows, as Hitler might speak of the gangsters in Chicago. "We Bolshevists," he said to me, "have always been interested in those heroes of popular legend because they represented the primitive revolt of the peasants against their oppressors. But riots of that kind lead to nothing. A peasants' revolt can only succeed if it is linked up with the workers' revolt and is under its leadership. Only *organized* revolt can reach its goal. In themselves, the peasants form no independent class."

The disappointing thing in statements of this kind, which are perfectly right in themselves, is the pedantic logic, the bookish tone in which Stalin pronounces them. He is to an uncanny degree a disciple of Hegel, who has been studied by every revolutionary from Lassalle and Marx to Lenin. Obviously a punishment of Hegel in Hades for having let his genius wither, at the end of his life, in the arid steppes of nationalism. Everything Stalin says is built up in Hegelian form on thesis, antithesis and synthesis, everything is confirmed by figures and percentages, and in the end every sum goes out without a remainder. The problem is solved, but it is lying lifeless on the floor. Clear-thinking and slow-moving, heavy and taciturn, this man with the slow, rather dragging gait and the averted eyes has nothing of Mussolini's highly personal way of seeing and showing the gulf which yawns between conclusions and their reasons.

III

For four years, Stalin was put definitely out of the way. When he was at last caught in 1913—it was at a meeting, and his friends had tried in vain to dress him in women's clothes in another room—the police, mindful of his five escapes, kept a much more careful eye on him; and until the Revolution broke out, he remained in Northern Siberia. During all those years, he was separated from his wife, whom he later divorced in the middle of the Civil War, in order to marry the younger daughter of a friend.

An amazing silence lies over those years, not only because he made no further attempt to escape, but also because he was in the end released by events in which, during all that time, he had had no hand. This time, it is true, the dreary prison village lay near the Arctic Circle, and this time he was surrounded by a special guard. There, in a marshy land lashed by snowstorms in winter, hunting geese and ducks and developing the art of patience by fishing in the summer, he kept house and cooked for himself. There Stalin lived until his thirty-eighth year, hearing of the outbreak of war but nothing of its progress. At first he had read Marx and Lenin with a friend, but the two soon came to hate each other in their wilderness, always waiting, always listening.

When at last, in March 1917, Kerensky's revolution opened all the prisons, Stalin went home, but not, like Lenin and Trotsky, as the wildly welcomed leader of the morrow. He had to wait still seven years more for that. Patience is his great quality. People who forget no insult, who are secretly moved by resentment and lust of revenge, men slow of gait and look, men who laugh dully, are either endowed with patience by fate, or practice it until they have learned to wait for their great moments.

In addition to patience, this unscrupulous man has more than his share of the personal courage which all the Russian leaders have shown. One critical evening at that time, in July 1917, when the sailors wanted to revolt and Lenin thought the moment premature, he sent his adjutant Stalin into the fortress of St. Peter and St. Paul to prevent the storm. Such a road is a road of life and death, and in retrospect loses nothing because it was taken in vain: The sailors began the fight, lost it, and Stalin had to take flight with Lenin and the others. For his obedience Lenin praised him now and then in letters, but always with moderation. Another proof that men, whether in power or in love, become accustomed only too soon to unconditional loyalty, and underestimate what they will never again have to conquer.

In the distribution of high positions, when the Party had actually come to power in October, Lenin gave Stalin only a second-rate post, namely the People's Commissarship for Nationality, while Trotsky, as minister for Foreign Affairs, was carving for himself a place at Lenin's side almost as his co-ruler.

At this point there began the ten years' struggle between the two men whose names have been most often pronounced in the world after that of Lenin. Lenin, whom I did not know, and of whom I can only form an idea by pictures, descriptions and documents, was obviously superior to both; a man both fiery and rational, resolute and flexible. Yet I have a right, based on my experience with each, to compare Trotsky, whom I visited in exile, with Stalin, with whom I had at any rate a very long conversation.

Trotsky's face bears all the marks of the passions bred in him by events. His eyes and forehead betray an interesting disharmony. Stalin, in whom both passion and disharmony are quite in the background, has a face less molded by fate. His forehead is strikingly low, his eyes always averted, partly out of embarrassment and partly out of craftiness. It is true that both faces bear the furrows which are the fingerprints of fate. Trotsky's face is not finished; his inward contradictions and tensions keep him young and restless. Stalin's heavy head makes a concentrated, but not very attractive picture. The only physical feature they have in common is their beautiful hands; I have seen such hands in all dictators.

Their characters confirm their physiognomies. On the one hand the mobile and highly educated son of a wealthy Jewish farmer, on the other the massive son of a poor cobbler, who got his education when his youth was past. Trotsky, like Lassalle, much-travelled, receptive, something of a poet, something of a Platonist, one of the most brilliant writers of our day—Stalin always working in the dark, inartistic, predominantly logical. One shares Lenin's fire, the other his thoroughness. Trotsky has the emotion, the élan of the speaker; Stalin the dangerous weight of the silent. Trotsky has spirit, Stalin patience. The one all too candid, the other all too reserved. Everything about Trotsky is agile, he speaks without notes. Everything about Stalin is leaden, he reads his speeches.

I should like to call Trotsky a messenger, Stalin a guardian. If Trotsky resembles a dashing chauffeur, who finds his way through every obstacle of traffic, I might compare Stalin to one of those tractors he has introduced into his country which, moving relentlessly forward, plough up the earth, hurl it aside, and cast in new seed at the same time—heavy, inexorable, rolling over everything in their path.

A clash between these two men, in such a time of anarchy, in the cramped and sudden circumstances of the Revolution, was simply inevitable. The only man who could reconcile them was Lenin. The perpetual complaints of one of his collaborators about the other, which are familiar to us in their letters, were cautiously settled by Lenin. Trotsky, with his streaks of genius, had a contempt for Stalin he found it difficult to conceal, and called him "the most eminent mediocrity of our Party." Stalin, in his turn, could not but distrust the adroit and voluble character of Trotsky. Lenin needed them both, although both threatened him with their resignations during the Civil War unless the other gave way. When Stalin, the commandant, gave a brilliant performance in the fighting round Tsaritsin, Trotsky, as Minister of War and Field Marshal, was of another opinion and demanded Stalin's recall. Lenin left Stalin at his post.

Yet Lenin's natural liking for Trotsky was impeded by the fact that the latter had, until the outbreak of the Revolution, remained his greatest Party enemy, and a Menshevik at all times. As such, Trotsky had fallen under the suspicion of the oldest revolutionaries. On the other hand, Lenin was attracted by Trotsky's genius; the culture of the two men and their lives abroad brought them together naturally. The perpetual contradictions of Trotsky had such a stimulating effect on Lenin as a ruler, that the efficiency and blind obedience of Stalin could not but pale in comparison. It was an historical necessity that two born intellectuals should lead the first revolution of the workers, but that a born worker should follow them in the work of consolidation. In the course of events, the Stalins always follow the Trotskys.

In the fighting on the southern Russian front at Tsaritsin, now called Stalingrad, the success of the whole campaign depended on safeguarding the supplies of corn. While Stalin, in contrast to Trotsky, was too suspicious to accept the assistance of Czarist officers, necessity soon made of him a general conducting war on his own account. In actual fact, both men had been civilians till the eve of the fighting. In this instance, Stalin is said to have cast aside the whole plan of action against Denikin in a report of seventy lines, and thereby won the victory against Trotsky's plans. What must Trotsky have thought as he saw his orders disregarded by his subordinate Stalin? Fortunately for his ego, he never knew that the latter had written across one of his telegrams: "Take no notice!"

But what must Stalin have felt as he watched Trotsky's fame and reputation growing steadily, while nobody spoke of him? The world was ringing with Trotsky's exploits, and history has ascribed to him, personally, the victory over the White forces. That was the man who, apparently an idle scribbler, spent his days dawdling in a café in Vienna just before the war. Count Berchtold, a man as silly as he was arrogant, the innocent author of the World War, said at the time: "What? I afraid of the Russian Socialists? What kind of men have they got? People like Mr. Braunstein Trotsky in the Café Central, I suppose." And this same dawdler created the Red Army under terrible conditions, in the midst of famine, anarchy and attacks by the Western world, and, by entrusting him with the leadership of that Army, Lenin put the armed forces of the country into his hands.

Repeatedly, however, the Revolution brought together the two men who hated each other, and when, in the spring of 1919, they had saved Petrograd from the attack by General Yudenich, even against the advice of Lenin, who wished to surrender the city, the highest decorations were conferred on both. Yet, although both were among the eight members of the Politbureau after the Civil War, Stalin had again to be satisfied with a second-rate office, while Trotsky was in the eyes of the world at Lenin's side.

Two years later, however, Lenin made his most faithful coadjutor General Secretary of the Communist Party. He needed a man of unconditional devotion there, where decisive power was concentrated, while he himself, by an unwritten law, had become dictator. This appointment, coming at the age of forty-two, was the beginning of Stalin's power. The man who had spent his life in constructive and active work, among the intrigues and sects of the party, who knew more comrades than Lenin and Trotsky put together, could now use his personal knowledge to guide the countless elections to the Soviets, great and small. For this purpose, he joined forces with Zinoviev and Kamenev, and the three together were nicknamed by the party "The Troika." His best instrument, however, was his friend and secretary, Molotov, who was as devoted to him as he to Lenin.

IV

Suddenly, Lenin fell ill under the enormous strain of these five years. He was half-paralyzed, was unable to speak for a long time. His mind, however, was quite unimpaired and at irregular intervals he would express views or give orders. When he returned to office for a short time a year later, he was startled. The Troika had taken all power into its own hands, and Stalin, the Party Secretary, was the real master of the situation. At that time Lenin wrote a letter to Trotsky which later became famous, telling him that he, Trotsky, should himself carry out an important mission to Georgia, Stalin's native province, instead of Stalin who had already been charged with it. He also wrote Stalin an angry letter breaking with him because of his boorishness to everybody and especially to Lenin's wife. This was later confirmed by Lenin's wife. Stalin never mentioned it. From that time on they were irreconcilable enemies. Lenin's widow is the only person in Russia who can criticize the dictator with impunity.

When Lenin died a year later, in January 1924, the Russian people felt instinctively that they were losing a great leader. The pilgrims to his lying-in-state came from every part of Russia, in the middle of winter, and in such countless numbers that the party members commissioned a chemist to preserve his body by artificial means for a few days. It was not until later that the idea occurred to them of embalming the dead leader permanently. The scientist who succeeded in doing so told me the story in detail. Today, Lenin's mausoleum before the walls of the Kremlin is more impressive than the tombs of kings.

Lenin left behind him a letter that may be regarded as his will, which was put into Stalin's hands and which he tried in vain to conceal. Since then a rough summary of it has been repeatedly published abroad in practically always the same terms. In this letter Lenin named as his possible successors only Stalin and Trotsky, but added:

"The grave danger in the relations between the two men is above all that of a Party split. Stalin, as General Secretary, has great power. I am not, however, sure that he always uses it circumspectly. Trotsky possesses not only unusual capacities—he is personally without question the most able man in the present committee—but possesses also excessive self-confidence and a tendency to over-emphasize the purely official aspect of things . . . His non-Bolshevist past is not a mere matter of chance . . . This difference between the two most able leaders might lead to a breach, even against their will." Postscript: "Stalin is too ruthless, and even though this fault is quite bearable among us Communists, it becomes unbearable in the General Secretary's office. Hence I propose that a way should be found to remove Stalin from that position and to give it to another, who, however, must differ from Stalin only in being better, namely more patient, loyal, polite, more attentive to his comrades and less moody. These things, which look like trifles, may one day be of crucial importance."

The nineteen members of the Committee at that time, as Radek told me, gathered soon after Lenin's death, anxious to hear what last advice their leader would give them from his glass coffin. Stalin read the letter aloud. No one stirred. When Trotsky's non-Bolshevist past was mentioned, he interrupted, asking: "What was that?" Stalin reread the sentence. Those were the only words spoken in that solemn hour.

Trotsky contests this text of the will and says that the sentence about his past ran quite differently, namely thus: "I should like to remind you that the October episode of Zinoviev was, of course, no mere matter of chance, but that it must no more be used for personal attacks than the fact of Trotsky's non-Bolshevist past."

In any case, Lenin's judgment and warning seem to have come from a man no longer in complete control of his powerful mind, for the warning caused great anxiety without giving any clear directions. The Party Congress passed over this last testament of Lenin in the speeches a few months later, and confirmed Stalin as General Secretary. And now the two rivals had to govern side by side. Soon the struggle for power began, in a journalistic duel on the surface, but behind the scenes, in Stalin's systematic undermining of Trotsky's fame and position among the soldiers and workmen. The struggle lasted five years, and, for the benefit of the outside world, was disguised as a quarrel about the form in which the Revolution was to go on.

In principle, the two men wanted the same thing: an industrial state and the expropriation of privately-owned land. Trotsky had the workmen on his side at the beginning, Stalin the peasants, or part of them, at the end. It was their rate of work which distinguished the two characters and hence the form of government they recommended. The peasants, 85% of all Russians, had been given their own land, the first and greatest success of the Revolution. Trotsky himself said to me: "It is possible that the Czars will come back. What seems impossible is that the peasants should lose their land!" At that time, however, Trotsky cried, chiefly as an attack on Stalin: "We have not made the Revolution in the towns in order to found a new capitalism in the country! The revolution is permanent." Stalin replied: "What we need is an interim solution, like Lenin's occasional return to private trade, which he himself called serious and durable. In his precipitateness, Trotsky is like a bad gardener, grasping a plant at the top of its stem and attempting to pull it out of the earth."

What becomes clear here is that there were two theories of the method in which Russia could reach the same goal, but at a different rate of progress. With his permanent revolution, Trotsky sought a link with world economy, for he regarded the autarchy of a single country as an impossibility. Stalin's slower reform aims to make Russia so independent in twenty years, by mobilizing all raw materials and transforming all agriculture into factories, that in the end this socialistic state will be able to underbid all the others, throw them all into confusion and so extend the world revolution to every citadel of capitalism. In this theory, he takes his stand on Lenin's order to extend the revolution only when at least one other country in Europe had become Socialist. He is fond of quoting Lenin's famous definition: "Communism is the power of the Soviets plus the electrification of the whole country." Hence the Five Year Plans, one of the most colossal of all state enterprises ever undertaken and admirable even if not an immediate and complete success. The moment that the official chief of the Five Year Plan, in the presence of a group of Party leaders, switched on one light after another on a gigantic map of Russia to show the mines, streets and dams, factories and cross-country cables then contemplated, and since then partly completed, was a great one in Russian history. The storm of applause which greeted the final glow over the whole map expressed the hopes of the potentially richest of nations, until then held in darkness and ruled by greed.

This mania for mechanizing everything, which terrifies us individualists, but which is Stalin's ruling passion, is also the explanation of his feeling for the United States. When I asked him how a purely socialistic state could admire the most highly capitalized one (this was in 1931, before Roosevelt) Stalin replied:

"We by no means admire America indiscriminately; we have a great admiration for American practicalness. Even though they are capitalists, they are healthy, or at any rate, there are a great many people in America who are healthy of mind and body in their whole attitude to things, to work. That industry and simplicity appeals to us. And in spite of everything, their customs in industry and economics are far more democratic than anywhere in Europe. It is a land of colonizers, without landowners and aristocrats. Hence the vigor of their customs. Our workers who have become economic leaders feel it at once. In America you can hardly distinguish an engineer from a mechanic when both are at work."

That was his task,—the complete, rapid, yet in point of fact, relatively slow reorganization of a vast country; and its leader seemed born to carry it out. Trotsky said something that historically seemed true when he admitted to me:

"It's always the same. After the first pioneers, the true revolutionaries, comes a second group, a series of second-rate men, who consolidate what the others have created."

He said that to me in his wretched, draughty wooden house on the island of Antigone in the sea of Marmora, a few sea miles away from Stamboul. He spoke in his peculiar, beautiful, high voice in the presence of his wife, who had followed our conversation gravely and in silence, and whose close communion with him in all the vicissitudes of fate is clearly apparent. Trotsky, who has studied a great deal of history, may have thought in his solitude of the fate of Themistocles, of Alcibiades, of Kimon, of Aristides, who had made Athens great only to be banished.

And yet Trotsky could have given affairs another turn. After Lenin's death, when Stalin took the party leadership into his hands, when he cast his net ever wider, and drew it ever closer, Trotsky, the chief and darling of the army, could have usurped possession of the ultimate power by a *coup d'état*. But there was nothing Napoleonic about him, and, like Bolivar, he passionately eschewed the imitation of everything that has made Napoleon an object of suspicion to all freeminded men. Hence he took up his pen, not his sword, though probably thinking, like Danton: *Ils n'oseront pas!*

He was mistaken. They *did* dare. Stalin managed first to hold him aloof, then to make his position untenable. The Politbureau, which was devoted to him, and later the Party

Congress, which Stalin had made his own faithful organ with almost Hitlerian skill, deprived Trotsky of his army command and gave him a position in the economic administration. He was openly reproached with having betrayed Leninism, and in a short time, the only person of importance to stand by him was the widow of Lenin himself.

Meanwhile there were conspiracies, just as in Czarist times. These men had learned all the methods and means by which they had themselves been persecuted, and now applied them to their own political opponents. At the celebration of the tenth anniversary of the Revolution, to the success of which no living man had contributed more than Trotsky, a soldier fired into his car, a workman broke its windows. The whole persecution, from the petty annoyances to the dreadful trials by which Stalin later annihilated his rivals, went on in true Russian style, that is, in accordance with the semi-Asiatic manners and morals which have prevailed there for centuries. One can only understand and partially excuse those inhuman acts when one thinks that this country had never known freedom, and that the goal of a new and utterly transformed country had to be attained by those very methods of violence which were the custom of the country.

It is from that point of view that I, too, try to understand the horrible trials in which the head of a state delivered his oldest friends up to death for crimes which, even though premeditated, were not directed against the work and the ideal of the Socialist revolution, but against its temporary leader and his methods. For the confessions of the accused, which were even more humiliating than the accusations themselves, I can find no explanation.

There was only one man Stalin did not venture to accuse and kill—Trotsky. Soon after the festival of the anniversary, Stalin first expelled his enemy from the Party, then exiled him. When Trotsky refused to obey, he had to be forcibly carried to a car by the police. Even then, Stalin expelled him from Siberia, that meant out of the territory of the Union, and finally, since nobody would have him, disposed of him with the Turks. A public trial would have been possible. The banishment was an act of truly Hitlerian ignominy.

Stalin, however, was shrewd enough to retire in victory; for that matter, he is not addicted to any form of exhibitionism. He is satisfied with the feeling of power, he does not need its outward appearance. He seldom shows himself in public, rarely speaks about himself, and always takes cover behind the Party Committee, of which he is only the secretary. In the struggle with his rivals he is satisfied with revenge. He needs no political dramatics.

V

Anyone driving into the Kremlin is received by Napoleon. A golden N is engraved on the mouth of each of the hundreds of cannon which are set there, the booty from the Emperor's invasion. The casual inspection by the sentinels at the entrance, which seemed to me humiliatingly brief—I could have had any kind of weapon with me, or been someone else—surprised me as much as it had in Rome. My friends tell me that people regard me everywhere as a pacifist and draw the false conclusion that I cannot shoot.

There the dictator occupies two plain rooms in an annex. His living quarters in another part of the Kremlin, where he lives with his family, is just as unpretentious. His office looks more like the hygienic surgery of a doctor, and the man in the light gray jacket, a kind of military tunic without buttons or badges, also looks thoroughly washed. Everything stands in precise and tasteless order on the long table, the carafes, ashtrays and sheets of paper. If Marx's magnificently domed forehead, which always reminds me of someone dear to me, did not look down from the wall, one might feel himself in Department X of the Y ministry in the capital of Z.

The slight embarrassment which a visitor from the West causes this dictator sits quite well on so powerful a man. For he sees practically nobody. On one occasion, I was thoroughly amused and surprised by the ambassadors of two great powers, who have been working in Moscow for years, who sent me an invitation in order to hear "what he was really like." The extreme simplicity which is his distinguishing characteristic would be a matter of course in a man of intelligence if he ran no risk of megalomania. For the cult carried on about him is as ridiculous as that in Rome and Berlin. Hence, when I asked him why he tolerated the busts and photographs in all the shopwindows in contradiction to the Marxian theory that the masses, not individuals, make history, he replied:

"You are mistaken! Your own theory, namely that individuals make history, stands in Marx's *Poverty of Philosophy*. Yet not in the way the imagination conceives, but according to the circumstances into which those men are born. Great men are only valuable in proportion to their grasp of circumstances; otherwise they become Don Quixotes. For that matter, Marx does not contrast men and circumstances; he never denied the role of the hero. So far as I can judge, men certainly make history."

When I then asked him whether an individual was not governing in Russia, instead of a committee, he pointed to the 16 chairs round our table and said: "Three revolutions have taught us that of every 100 decisions an individual makes, 90 are wrong. Our committee of seventy members comprises the most intelligent leaders of industry, the shrewdest business men, the most skillful agitators, experts in agriculture and nationality. Each one of them can correct a single resolution by his experience."

"But if in this building you are so democratic," I objected, "why is your government so cruel, at the end of fourteen years, that everybody in your country fears you?"

To this challenge—for I had made up my mind to be

rough and discourteous in the Kremlin—Stalin made a long, quiet reply on the history of the Bolsheviks, whose beginnings were far too mild, and said, at the end of his discussion, that my mistake in this matter was a general one. "Do you really believe a man could maintain his position of power for fourteen years merely by intimidation? Only by making people afraid? The Czars were pastmasters of that art and what has become of them? Fear is a question of the mechanics of administration. You can excite fear for a year or two. But not among our peasants! Our workmen and peasants are not so timid as you think. If Europe, forming its judgment by its experiences with the Old Russian landowners who amused themselves in Paris, imagines our people to be lazy, it underestimates their determination to be understood by their leader. Plekhanov, who once had the greatest authority over his followers, was quickly forgotten by the crowd when his politics began to limp. Trotsky, also a man of great authority, was forgotten. And if he is remembered, it is only with a feeling of rage."

As Stalin stopped at this point, and with his indefatigable red pencil made a rapid, vicious and illegible sign which Oriental priests would interpret as a curse, I went on inquiring about Trotsky.

"If you take the active workmen," Stalin now replied with amazing coolness, "nine-tenths of them now speak of him with anger and bitterness. You ask about fear? Well, a small part of the peasants, the kulaks, are afraid.

They are afraid of the other peasant groups. But there were similar antipathies among the old bourgeoisie and among the tradesmen. Of the adult peasants and workmen, 15% at the most keep silence through fear. Besides, our workmen have three revolutions behind them, that is sufficient practice for them to destroy leaders they do not like."

Later when I turned the conversation to the astonishing *volte-face* in which the communism of recent years cast all its boasted equality behind it, Stalin made a long and doctrinaire reply. He described a perfectly Socialist society as an impossibility so long as classes existed, and so long as work was a burden for many, and pleasure for only a few.

" 'Every man according to his abilities and attainments'; that is the Marxist formula for the first stage of socialism. In the final stage, every man will produce as much as he can and be paid according to his needs. Socialism has never denied differences in tastes and needs, the extent of such differences. Why, Marx attacks the principle of absolute equality! In the West, people imagine that we want first to collect everything, then distribute it in a thoroughly primitive fashion. That might do for Cromwell, but not for our scientific socialism."

VI

And yet it is the old revolutionary ideas which guide Stalin on, as Lenin was guided by them. When a revolutionary has steadily pursued the same goal for forty years, one could expect a transformation of his views only if they jeopardized his position. Actually, Stalin, like every other dictator, would be a dead man if he went back on himself. Hitler can emphasize now nationalism, now socialism, and take each in turn as his goal, since both are contained in the name of his Party. Mussolini, too, has a considerable margin for play with his economic forms, and he has used every bit of it. Stalin may be able to suppress the freedom of his workmen; he can never confront them with another class enjoying greater rights and a higher income. He cannot in any way restore the class system, nor does he want to.

We do not know what his enemies are preparing against him. He replied to a series of assassinations with the kidnapping and murder of his chief White Russian enemy in Paris, who was apparently the motivating force behind the assassinations. But if Stalin has nothing in mind but his personal power, that is all the more reason why he should remain Socialist. For if the people, who are more afraid of him than he will admit, desired another system, it would choose leaders of quite a different kind.

Hence, his alliance with capitalistic Germany is quite different from Mussolini's alliance with capital. Mussolini began his road to power with a *volte-face*, he founded his Party and his army on a new doctrine quite alien to socialism. He took this turn as early as 1915, when he was 30. Stalin, on the other hand, has changed nothing in his régime which Lenin or even Trotsky would not have changed in the same sense. His alliance with Germany, which he concluded at the age of 60, I can only explain as an intermediate landing on a long flight.

There is only one decisive difference—the purposes they serve. If Stalin wishes nothing but a Russia extending over as many square miles as under the Czars, he is simply a little Hitler. In that case he misjudges the spirit of his age just as crassly as Hitler, for the spirit of these times is directed no longer toward world empire, but toward state socialism. Yet such a misjudgment is refuted by his whole life, his doctrine, his heredity, even his mistakes.

Having extended his country by his latest conquests without a battle,—we are referring to Poland, not Finland —and so fired the imagination of the millions under him, whose fathers told them stories of Russian Riga, Stalin is out to win the affection of those whom fear keeps silent, and who comprise not 15%, but 50% or even more of the population. Since he has now been at his work of reconstruction for over ten years, and has made Russia not only independent, but for the first time in its history, is making it a great export country, he can hope to touch the Western world more quickly and more definitely with the growing length of his feelers. It cannot be the intention of a man so fanatical, so logical and yet so patient, it cannot be the intention of such a passionate disciple of Lenin and Marx, to betray both and make common cause with the Fascists. His real object can only be to overcome them.

Every intelligent reader of the world press realized that Hitler and Stalin were out to cheat one another as soon as possible, when they concluded their pacts. What everybody does not know, however, is that Stalin stands a far better chance of winning the great game. When I asked him about ambition, and whether it impeded or promoted energy, he replied:

"That varies. In certain circumstances it can act as a stimulant. Generally it is a hindrance for a person's fate."

"Fate?" I returned. "Do you believe in fate?"

Then he stiffened suddenly, looked at me for the first time with wide-open eyes, and paused for the first time. Then he said in a hard voice:

"No. I do not believe in fate. It is a prejudice. The notion is nonsense. Fate: as among the Greeks, when there were gods and goddesses directing everything from above. I don't believe in such mysticism. There are reasons why I was not killed in the war. But someone else might quite well be sitting here in my place."

Such a man is stronger than his mystical and hysterical opposite.

POSTSCRIPT

WHEN I COMPARE THE THREE DICTATORS, I SEE first a common will to power which suffers no scruples, annihilates every enemy, knows no morality, mercy or chivalry. Hence the end of freedom for all they govern, the stifling of all virile contradiction, the contempt for the masses, the persecution of intellect.

Yet the three differ in their relation to the State. Hitler and Mussolini, without fundamental constitutional ideas, without training or dogma, are ready to introduce any form of society which will preserve their power. Stalin, the only dictator to succeed another, works out the forms transmitted to him by others, and which he can never betray. The first two, therefore, are more in the class of adventurers and gamblers than Stalin.

Comparing their characters, the three men share three deep-seated traits: a small capacity for love, a great capacity for hate, and an eminent and unquenchable belief in themselves. Other traits divide them into three groups:

Stalin and Hitler have in common both their predominant passion for revenge, which seems somewhat weaker in Mussolini, and their lack of culture.

Stalin and Mussolini share courage, patience, realism, sexual normality, contempt of money. Hitler possesses none of these five traits.

Hitler and Mussolini have in common their vanity, lack of humor, superstition, contempt for the crowd and for the ideal they pretend to serve. These five qualities are alien to Stalin.

Hence of the three, Stalin is the only man of conviction, Mussolini the only strong personality, and Hitler the only lunatic.

From their characters and the general situation within their countries, we can deduce their futures. Leaving out of account unpredictable assassinations or illnesses, since such things usually have no historical necessity, we can assume that, at the end of the war, Stalin will still be in power, Mussolini only if he remains neutral, and Hitler in no case.

Their position in the eyes of history may be on similar lines. The man who has transformed Russia is sure of his place. It is more important and more significant to awaken a half-sleeping multitude than to take a highly-developed country a step further in technology. But a man who extends the frontiers of his country without founding a new idea or culture, can achieve glory only as a great personality. A victory won by Hitler could be maintained by the Germans for only ten years; a victory by Mussolini could not be maintained by the Italians for three. Hence if all three were conquered, it would mean the salvation of all their three nations.

Since the war must end with the restoration of personal freedom within these countries, and with the union of Europe abroad, the world will turn away in disgust from all tribunes of the people who have founded their power on drums and processions, photographs and radio speeches. People will repudiate as bad taste the advertisement in government which has degraded politics. The three dictators, who had to deprive millions of their freedom and life to come to self-awareness, will be as quickly forgotten as Napoleon III, who was for 20 years more powerful than any of them. When the names of Hitler, Mussolini and Stalin have long been forgotten outside of their own countries, the world will still be speaking of Zeppelin, Marconi and Gorki.

Power and influence, after the war, will again fall to the statesman who is less of an actor and more of an expert, less of an orator and more of a specialist. The atmosphere of the circus and the cinema surrounding the dictators of our day will yield to that of a well-ventilated government room, in which men will once more negotiate in peace instead of threatening and, instead of bullying, will even dare to laugh.